LET
Earth
RECEIVE HER
KING

An Advent Devotional

Copyright © 2020 by The Foundry Publishing
The Foundry Publishing
PO Box 419527
Kansas City, MO 64141
thefoundrypublishing.com

978-0-8341-3892-6

Printed in the
United States of America

Cover Design: J.R. Caines (Caines Design)
Interior Design: J.R. Caines (Caines Design)

The internet addresses, email addresses, and phone numbers in this book
are accurate at the time of publication. They are provided as a resource.
The Foundry Publishing does not endorse them or vouch for their content
or permanence.

10 9 8 7 6 5 4 3 2

CONTENTS

AN INVITATION TO RECEIVE

The Old Testament tells the story of three exiles. The third—and most recent of the three—is the exile of Judah in Babylon. In 587 BCE, Nebuchadnezzar took the best and brightest of Judah into captivity, separating God's people across the empire and hoping to repopulate the conquered cities. Like Jonah stuck in the belly of the great fish, Judah should have died in exile. But, also like Jonah, God refused to let death have the final say. After more than forty years of waiting, the Lord sent a king—Cyrus the Persian—to set the captive Judeans free and let them return to Jerusalem.

As the newly released captives compiled their history and narrated their surprising deliverance, they realized that the story of exile and divine liberation was not just Judah's story but, looking back, it was also the story of the entire nation of Israel. The second exile story is the one of Israel's captivity as slaves in the land of Egypt under the authoritarian and violent rule of Pharaoh. Slaves have no hope and no future. However, God heard the cries of Abraham's descendants and sent a deliverer—a prophet named Moses—to bring down mighty Pharaoh and lead the people through the waters of new life.

As those Judean historians looked back across time, they realized there was one last story of exile to tell. Exile is not just the story of Judah and of Israel; it is also the story of the whole creation. In the beginning, humankind lived in a blessed land—a garden—in harmony with God and God's purposes. Sin, however, fractured humankind's relationship with God, with one another, with the land, and even with other humans. Evicted from the garden, Adam and Eve represented all of creation tumbling, without hope, into exile.

Judah was redeemed by Cyrus. Israel was set free by Moses. But who could possibly lead *all of creation* out of exile? Each year at Christmas, the church celebrates that, in Jesus Christ, God has heard the world's cries and has sent a king, a prophet, a savior to redeem creation. Each year at Easter, the church proclaims that, in the life, death, and resurrection of this redeemer, Jesus, the exile of creation created by sin, evil, darkness, and death has been defeated by the grace, goodness, light, and resurrection life of Christ. So what is the church doing at Advent?

In Advent, God's people fast in preparation for the final feast. The church finds itself caught between times. The world's true King has already come. If anyone is in Christ, their exile is over. That person is already part of the new creation (2 Cor. 5:17). At Christmas, followers of Jesus celebrate that creation's long-expected redemption has arrived. **Let earth receive her King**.

However, the reign of the King has not yet come in all its fullness, which means that times reminiscent of exile still persist. Things are not yet the way they are supposed to be. In response, God's people fast and wait and pray. Together, the church prays, "Come quickly, Lord Jesus. Come, and make all things new!" **Let earth receive her King**.

And so we wait. But we do not wait like people sitting bored at the DMV or the doctor's office, riffling through outdated magazines, frustratedly anticipating our name to be called. Rather, the church waits actively, like a parent preparing for the coming of a child, making everything at home ready for the new arrival.

In the waiting, we are changed. In the great Christmas hymn "Joy to the World," the line that follows the title of this book is, "Let every heart prepare him room." During Advent, the church practices four virtues that grow in us, preparing room for the new creation to come in its fullness. Those virtues are hope, peace, joy, and love. Traditionally, each of those virtues is highlighted, one by one, during the four weeks of Advent.

This devotional follows that pattern and centers on those virtues. The Sunday scriptures are taken from the Revised Common Lectionary for Year B. The devotional thought for Sundays is a bit lengthier to help those who are preaching, teaching, and gathering in small groups around those weekly texts. The daily readings are shorter and more personal and center on the four virtues of hope, peace, joy, and love, with space for individual prayer and reflection each day.

In preparing this guide, my hope and prayer has been that the Lord would use it to help those taking this journey to prepare room for the coming of the King and the in-breaking of his new creation today, as well as his ultimate eventual return.

Blessings,

T. Scott Daniels

*Hope is nothing else than the expectation of those
things which faith has believed to have been truly
promised by God. Thus, faith believes God to be
true, believes that he is our Father; hope anticipates
that he will ever show himself to be a Father toward
us; faith believes that eternal life has been given
to us, hope anticipates that it will some time be
revealed; faith is the foundation upon which hope
rests, hope nourishes and sustains faith. . . . Thus in
the Christian life faith has the priority, but hope the
primacy. Without faith's knowledge of Christ, hope
becomes a utopia and remains hanging in the air.*

—JURGEN MOLTMANN,
A Theology of Hope

HOPE

First Sunday of Advent
November 29, 2020

SCRIPTURE READINGS

PSALM 80; **ISAIAH 64:1–9**; MARK 13:24–37;
1 CORINTHIANS 1:3–9

Oh, that you would rend the heavens and come down, that the mountains would tremble before you! As when fire sets twigs ablaze and causes water to boil, come down to make your name known to your enemies and cause the nations to quake before you!

You come to the help of those who gladly do right, who remember your ways. But when we continued to sin against them, you were angry. How then can we be saved?

Yet you, Lord, are our Father. We are the clay, you are the potter; we are all the work of your hand. Do not be angry beyond measure, Lord; do not remember our sins forever. Oh, look on us, we pray, for we are all your people.

—ISAIAH 64:1–2, 5, 8–9

"It's all gone. What do we do now?"

Twice I have stood with friends after they lost everything. The first family had a tornado pick up everything they owned and scatter their possessions in places they could never be found. The other family watched a raging fire turn treasures and memories into ash—a lifetime gathered over decades, gone in a matter of minutes.

I hurt every time I see news reports of people who return home after a hurricane or a flood only to find rubble and chaos where there used to be security and peace.

The text from Isaiah for this first Sunday of Advent comes from a similar place of loss and disarray. The likely context is around the year 530 BCE, when—after nearly five decades of Babylonian exile—the Judeans were set free and sent home by Cyrus the Persian. For a generation, have dreamed about the day they would return home. They sang songs of joy all along the journey back to the holy city. Unfortunately, when they arrived back in Jerusalem, their joy quickly turned to sorrow when they found barrenness, destruction, and the need to start all over.

It's no wonder the prophet lifts his head to the sky and shouts a lament to God on behalf of the people. *Oh, that you would rend the heavens and come down!* The people need God to come down and—like a child shaking an Etch-a-Sketch and starting all over—rattle the earth and reorient the mountains. They need the energy of God's fire and the warmth of God's presence. They need God to scatter their enemies—who recognize how vulnerable they are—and bring them security and freedom from fear of the future. They want the glory days to return; the days when the world knew that God was active and present in the midst of God's chosen people. They long for a time when the glory of God seemed to reflect off every building, reverberate in every psalm of praise, and radiate out from Jerusalem like a healing wave of peace throughout the land.

The lament of the prophet quickly turns into a prayer of confession, though. The people sit in a pile of rubble with no hope to move forward—but it is rubble of their own making. They turned away from God's purposes. They misused their power. Their idolatry and disobedience reawakened the chaos they now drowned in.

In most Bible translations there is a double space between verses 7 and 8. It is as though biblical scholars recognize there is a space—a gap—that should fall there. It is a not a gap we should cross over too quickly. It is the gap of despair. It is the gap of dashed dreams. It is the gap of barrenness, emptiness, and destruction. It is the gap we too acknowledge and recognize as we enter into Advent.

However, the gap doesn't have the final word. Eventually, the first words of verse 8 break through: *Yet, you, Lord, are our Father*. That beautiful, glorious "yet" makes all the difference. That "yet" moves the action away from Judah and their brokenness and squarely onto God and God's presence, action, and character. It is the "yet" of Advent hope.

Our world can often be a place of deep darkness, brokenness and sin. Yet, God is a loving father working for the good of God's children. Yet, God is a genius potter making something beautiful out of our chaotic clay. Yet, God is a master builder crafting a new creation out of the leftover rubble of the world gone its own way.

This is where Advent begins—with the hope that those who lament in brokenness will hear the "yet" of the constantly re-creating God.

BLESSING FOR THE DAY

Show me your ways, Lord, teach me your paths. Guide me in your truth and teach me, for you are God my Savior, and my hope is in you all day long.

—PSALM 25:4–5

HYMN FOR THE WEEK

Pardon for sin and a peace that endureth,
Thine own dear presence to cheer and to guide;
Strength for today and bright hope for tomorrow,
Blessings all mine, with ten thousand beside!
"Great is thy faithfulness!"
"Great is thy faithfulness!"
Morning by morning, new mercies I see;
All I have needed thy hand hath provided;
"Great is thy faithfulness," Lord unto me!

QUESTIONS FOR DISCUSSION OR REFLECTION

1. As you begin this Advent season, what are the places in your life that feel or seem hopeless?

    _____

    _____

2. What would you like God to do? What would it look like for God to tear open the heavens and come down into your situation?

    _____

    _____

3. How have you seen God work in the past, or where has God been faithful to you?

    _____

    _____

4. Hope is different than optimism. Hope is confidence in God, not just the expectation that things will simply work out. What aspects of the character of God give you hope?

    _____

    _____

PRISONERS OF HOPE

SCRIPTURE READING

ZECHARIAH 9:9–12

See, your king comes to you, righteous and victorious, lowly and riding on a donkey, on a colt, the foal of a donkey.

Return to your fortress, you prisoners of hope; even now I announce that I will restore twice as much to you.

—ZECHARIAH 9:9b, 12

Several years ago, I stumbled across a television interview with the well-known academic and civil-rights advocate Cornel West. The interviewer asked Dr. West how he could stay so optimistic in his work on race relations when it always seems as though, as a culture, we seem to take two steps back from reconciliation for every step we take forward? In his uniquely beautiful and rhetorical way, Cornel West responded, "No. No. No. I am not optimistic or pessimistic. That is an attitude. I am a prisoner of hope!" I don't believe the interviewer knew that the prophet Zechariah had just been invoked, but I did.

The ministry of Zechariah arose approximately around the same time and in the same context as Sunday's text from Isaiah. The people of Judah have returned home only to find rubble around them and an overwhelming amount of work ahead of them. Besides the questions surrounding the rebuilding project, the question of leadership also needed to be addressed. Would there be a new king to lead this redeemed people?

Zechariah envisions a new king coming to Jerusalem, riding gently, as a healing presence to restore the people. Of course, these words that rang true in Zechariah's day became even more true a few centuries later when the humble King of the world also came humbly riding into Jerusalem on a donkey, thus fulfilling (or, maybe better, "filling full") Zechariah's prophetic expectation.

The line that always grabs me is Zechariah's call to "prisoners of hope." What an amazing image! He sees God's people as captured by hope in ways they simply cannot escape. They might despair if they could—but they simply can't. They are prisoners of hope that the God who called them and led them out of exile will be faithful to finish the work that he started.

I find myself needing to embrace that proclamation from Zechariah often. This is not the easiest age during which to live faithfully as God's people. I find myself—not only as a church leader but also simply as a believer—struggling with the temptation to despair. If you were to ask me how I stay so "optimistic" when it often seems in the church, and in my own journey, we too often take one step forward and two steps back, my answer would be: No, no, no. I am not optimistic or pessimistic. I am a prisoner of hope. I have been captured by the faithfulness of the humble yet conquering King, and I simply can't escape the hope that he who began this good work will carry it on to completion (Phil. 1:6).

BLESSING FOR THE DAY

Be strong and take heart, all you who hope in the Lord.

—PSALM 31:24

QUESTIONS FOR REFLECTION

1. What images or pictures come to mind when you think of Zechariah's great line, "prisoners of hope"?

   _____

   _____

   _____

   _____

2. How can you live today, not as optimistic or pessimistic, but as a prisoner of hope? What actions would a prisoner of hope in your circumstances take?

   _____

   _____

   _____

   _____

THOSE WHO HOPE IN THE LORD

TUESDAY, DECEMBER 1, 2020

SCRIPTURE READING

ISAIAH 40:1–5, 25–31

Comfort, comfort my people, says your God.

Do you not know? Have you not heard? The LORD is the everlasting God, the Creator of the ends of the earth. He will not grow tired or weary, and his understanding no one can fathom. He gives strength to the weary and increases the power of the weak. Even youths grow tired and weary, and young men stumble and fall; but those who hope in the LORD will renew their strength. They will soar on wings like eagles; they will run and not grow weary, they will walk and not be faint.

—ISAIAH 40:1, 28–31

I've had my share of church service interruptions. I've had the power go out during the sermon. Once, a young man suffering from schizophrenia started yelling at me from the congregation. I've had a fight break out between two people. A woman once ran onto the platform and stole the book I was reading from right out of my hands. I've even (yes, this is true) had a person die in the middle of the service. I'm waiting for the week the fire alarm goes off while I'm in the pulpit. It's only a matter of time.

Not all interruptions, however, are negative. Sometimes they can be just what was needed. It is believed that Isaiah chapters 40–55 were written while the Judeans were still in exile in Babylon. God's people were caught up in lamenting the reality of unending captivity when a marvelous interruption broke in. Their laments sounded like this:

> Bitterly [Jerusalem] weeps at night,
> tears are on her cheeks.
> Among all her lovers
> there is no one to comfort her.
>
> Her fall was astounding;
> there was none to comfort her.
>
> Zion stretches out her hands,
> but there is no one to comfort her.
>
> "People have heard my groaning,
> but there is no one to comfort me."
> (Lamentations 1:2a–b, 9b, 17a, 21a)

Did you catch the lament? There is no one to comfort, no one to comfort, no one to comfort.

Suddenly the prophet Isaiah interrupts! *Comfort, comfort my people, says your God.* Their laments are gloriously interrupted with a proclamation of hope—hope that God was bringing comfort, hope that God would bring them out of exile, hope that their exhaustion formed in despair might be reversed into unbridled, youthful energy.

Prisoners of hope are not exempt from times of lament. Prisoners of hope are not guaranteed freedom from exhaustion. However, prisoners of hope are promised times of renewal. God's people are continually reinvigorated by knowing that the Lord is everlasting, that the Creator does not grow tired or weary, and that God gives strength to the worn-out and power to the weak.

BLESSING FOR THE DAY

No king is saved by the size of his army; no warrior escapes by his great strength.

We wait in hope for the LORD; he is our help and our shield.

—PSALM 33:16, 20

QUESTIONS FOR REFLECTION

1. What are the places or things that are making you most weary and tired today? Offer those to God.

   _____

   _____

   _____

   _____

2. What are the ways you believe God wants to renew your strength?

   _____

   _____

   _____

   _____

3. How can you be the source of God's energy, renewal, encouragement, and strength right now for someone who is tired and weary?

   _____

   _____

   _____

   _____

PLANS TO GIVE YOU HOPE

WEDNESDAY, DECEMBER 2, 2020

SCRIPTURE READING

JEREMIAH 29:10–14

This is what the LORD says: "When seventy years are completed for Babylon, I will come to you and fulfill my good promise to bring you back to this place. For I know the plans I have for you," declares the LORD, "plans to prosper you and not to harm you, plans to give you hope and a future. Then you will call on me and come and pray to me, and I will listen to you. You will seek me and find me when you seek me with all your heart. I will be found by you," declares the LORD, "and will bring you back from captivity. I will gather you from all the nations and places where I have banished you," declares the LORD, "and will bring you back to the place from which I carried you into exile."

—JEREMIAH 29:10–14

I started working with college students about twenty-five years ago, and one thing I've learned in those twenty-five years is that college students *love* Jeremiah 29:11. I am convinced that God declaring he has prosperous plans for our future is every Christian college student's favorite biblical promise. They usually take it to mean that— before they graduate—God will get the perfect spouse, the perfect job, and the perfect living location all prepared and waiting for them.

Of course, few people ever pay attention to Jeremiah 29:10. *When seventy years are completed for Babylon, I will come to you and fulfill my good promise to bring you back to this place.* Seventy years! Seventy years! God says he'll get to the plans in *seventy* years! Verse 10 *never* makes it onto the t-shirts. I sometimes teasingly tell my students that God promises to get around to fulfilling those prosperous plans by the time they are ninety-two or ninety-three. So what do we do with God's delay? We do what Jeremiah says: we hope. We also learn patience.

In *The Patient Ferment of the Early Church*, Alan Kreider argues that, surprisingly, during the first three centuries of Christianity, there were very few sermons, letters, or tracts written about evangelism—or, what we would think of today as "church growth." However, there were lots of sermons, letters, and tracts written about developing the virtue of patience. In discussing the writings of the early church father Tertullian, Kreider writes, "According to Tertullian, impatient actions do not produce what they promise. Instead, impatient actions make things worse, bringing about massive misfortunes. . . . Patience on the other hand, brings new possibilities. Patience is the source of the 'practices of peace,' which bring reconciliation week by week.'"

Patience brings new possibilities. Jeremiah 29 is likely written around the same time as yesterday's text, Isaiah 40. The Judeans in exile didn't have to wait patiently for all seventy years of the Babylonian empire's powerful reign to be over. They only had to wait out the last forty years or so. Forty is an important number in Scripture. It rains on the earth in the Noah story for forty days. Moses spends forty days up on Mount Sinai receiving the Torah. The people wander in the post-Egyptian wilderness for forty years. And, of course, Jesus spends forty days in the desert being tempted by Satan to define the kingdom by some other way than the cross. In the Bible, forty is a number that signifies a time when significant transformation happens. No one comes out of "God's forty" the same as when they went in.

Hope allows God's people not just to endure life's moments of "forty," awaiting the glorious future but also to patiently receive the transformation that happens in the God-filled meantime.

BLESSING FOR THE DAY

Why, my soul, are you downcast? Why so disturbed within me? Put your hope in God, for I will yet praise him, my Savior and my God.

—PSALM 42:11

QUESTIONS FOR REFLECTION

1. God does not just ask God's people to be patient. God is patient also. What can we learn from the patience of God?

    _____

    _____

    _____

    _____

2. Are you in one of "God's forty" moments right now? What is God using this time to teach you, and how is God changing you along the way?

    _____

    _____

    _____

    _____

BUT IF WE HOPE

THURSDAY, DECEMBER 3, 2020

SCRIPTURE READING

ROMANS 5:1–5; 8:18–28

Therefore, since we have been justified through faith, we have peace with God through our Lord Jesus Christ, through whom we have gained access by faith into this grace in which we now stand. And we boast in the hope of the glory of God. Not only so, but we also glory in our sufferings, because we know that suffering produces perseverance; perseverance, character; and character, hope. And hope does not put us to shame, because God's love has been poured out into our hearts through the Holy Spirit, who has been given to us.

I consider that our present sufferings are not worth comparing with the glory that will be revealed in us.

For in this hope we were saved. But hope that is seen is no hope at all. Who hopes for what they already have? But if we hope for what we do not yet have, we wait for it patiently.

And we know that in all things God works for the good of those who love him, who have been called according to his purpose.

—ROMANS 5:1–5; 8:18, 24–25, 28

The Hebrew word for "glory" is *kavod* (pronounced with a long "o" like "abode"). It is a word that shows up frequently in Scripture, and it is associated with heaviness or weightiness. It is as though God's glory—the *kavod Yahweh*—is the indentation, or fingerprints, that God's presence leaves behind. My poor kids have heard me preach many sermons on the *kavod Yahweh*. I love when the presence of God changes the face of Moses and causes it to radiate God's glory. I love to think about God's glory descending and filling the newly constructed temple.

Several years ago, my oldest son, Caleb, and I were in the living room together doing our favorite thing: sitting in our beloved chairs, reading silently, while everyone else in the family was out making noise and creating chaos somewhere in the world. It was kind of a gray day outside, but the wind must have blown the clouds away because suddenly, like someone pulling open the shades across the windows, the sun came out and filled the living room. My young son looked up suddenly from his book and said, "Dad! The *kavod Yahweh*!" Indeed. It felt like the glory of God had just filled the room.

In the tenth chapter of Ezekiel, the prophet saw the glory of God depart from the temple as a consequence of exile. This moment is a tragic one for God's people. One of the great hopes of the Old Testament was that God would dwell uniquely in the midst of God's people and that God's glory would radiate out from Zion to the world, and the whole creation would be healed. At the end of the Old Testament the temple is being rebuilt, but the glory of God has yet to return. In fact, one of the questions that hangs over God's people as the New Testament begins is, will God's glory ever return and dwell once again in the midst of the people?

Of course, the Advent answer to that question is the one the Gospel of John proclaims: *The Word became flesh and made his dwelling* [literally, "tabernacled" or "templed") *among us. We have seen his glory, the glory of the one and only Son, who came from the Father, full of grace and truth* (John 1:14). The glory of God indeed did return to Jerusalem and even to the temple itself. But not everyone recognized that glory.

In Romans 5–8, Paul gives us his majestic manifesto on hope and glory. The great apostle is convinced that God's glory now resides in the new temple—the church—and slowly radiates out from the body of Christ, giving glimpses of that glory, until God's glory is fully revealed and the creation is made new. In the meantime, we are filled with the Spirit and are the firstfruits of that new creation.

However, we are not only a foretaste of the coming kingdom, but we are also groaners in the current one. For Paul, the whole creation is groaning like a mother in childbirth waiting for redemption; waiting for God's glory to be revealed. The groans of creation—and our groans as those who suffer and pray along with creation—are not primarily the grunts of pain but the sighs of those who, in hope, know God's glorious renewal is coming. Sometimes, as we look at the broken and often violent world around us, we want God's great re-creation to come so badly that we don't even know how to articulate our prayers. We can only groan in hope that the Spirit of God who also groans with creation hears and understands our hope-filled sighs.

This is why Advent hymns sound more like groans than like praise-filled anthems. "O Come, O Come, Emmanuel" and "Come, Thou Long-Expected Jesus" aren't the peppiest tunes out there. They are the mournful psalms of hopeful groaners who know that, ultimately, hope will not disappoint us.

BLESSING FOR THE DAY

Yes, my soul, find rest in God; my hope comes from him.

—PSALM 62:5

QUESTIONS FOR REFLECTION

1. List two or three places where you know the creation or the people within creation are groaning for redemption. Spend some time groaning to God for those people and those places.

    _____

    _____

    _____

    _____

2. What does it mean for you to groan in hope?

    _____

    _____

    _____

    _____

3. Where have you seen the glory of God—the fingerprints of God—in your life lately?

    _____

    _____

    _____

    _____

HOPE AS AN ANCHOR FOR THE SOUL

FRIDAY, DECEMBER 4, 2020

SCRIPTURE READING

HEBREWS 6:9–20

God is not unjust; he will not forget your work and the love you have shown him as you have helped his people and continue to help them. We want each of you to show this same diligence to the very end, so that what you hope for may be fully realized. We do not want you to become lazy, but to imitate those who through faith and patience inherit what has been promised.

We have this hope as an anchor for the soul, firm and secure. It enters the inner sanctuary behind the curtain, where our forerunner, Jesus, has entered on our behalf.

—HEBREWS 6:10–12, 19–20a

My parents and my sister's family were on a cruise together when suddenly, and without warning, the ship tilted to one side at almost a forty-five-degree angle. My family was in the dining room at the time. All the dishes went flying off tables, and the wait staff all fell to the ground. People started panicking and tried to get to the exits, but the tilt was actually too steep for most folk to get to the doors on the higher end of the ship. My dad said later that terrifying scenes from *Titanic* were flashing through his mind when, after a couple of minutes, the ship righted itself and the dinner—that they were now wearing—continued. It turned out to be a motor issue. (I just assumed the Lord was punishing them for not inviting my wife and me.)

I have been on a few, very uneventful, cruises. As the passengers come onboard, I always pay attention to the massive anchors held in place with enormous chains attached to the ship. They look, thankfully, unused. I can't imagine being in the kind of storm that would require a ship of that size to drop those anchors and try to keep that giant vessel in place. Even with those anchors, I can imagine the force and power of the waves pulling and tilting a ship that size in a storm.

First-century recipients of Scripture were likely familiar with anchors and how they operated. What is unusual in Hebrews is not that the writer would mention the use of an anchor, but where the anchor is grounded. It is fixed in the center of the temple (the place where, in yesterday's reading, the unique glory of God was found and then exited). However, for the writer of Hebrews, the believer's anchor of life is not fixed firm and secure in the old Holy of Holies but in the new one—the heavenly one, entered into by Christ through his death and resurrection.

What a powerful image! We are not left out in life floating on the sea, tossed wherever the wind may take us. We are anchored in the very presence of God. The promise—the hope—of Hebrews is not that we won't experience storms. In fact, the very idea that we may *need* an anchor all but guarantees that storms will indeed come. Our hope is that, though the storms of life may batter us, they cannot ultimately move us into places of destruction and devastation. Our anchor is fixed in the in-breaking and re-creating love of God.

BLESSING FOR THE DAY

Israel, put your hope in the LORD, for with the LORD is unfailing love and with him is full redemption.

—PSALM 130:7

QUESTIONS FOR REFLECTION

1. What does it mean for you to find your life anchored in Christ?

    _____

    _____

    _____

    _____

2. What are the promises of God that you find hope in today and find an anchor for your soul?

    _____

    _____

    _____

    _____

INTO A
LIVING HOPE

SATURDAY, DECEMBER 5, 2020

SCRIPTURE READING

1 PETER 1:3–9, 20–21

Praise be to the God and Father of our Lord Jesus Christ! In his great mercy he has given us new birth into a living hope through the resurrection of Jesus Christ from the dead.

In all this you greatly rejoice, though now for a little while you may have had to suffer grief in all kinds of trials. These have come so that the proven genuineness of your faith—of greater worth than gold, which perishes even though refined by fire—may result in praise, glory and honor when Jesus Christ is revealed.

He was chosen before the creation of the world, but was revealed in these last times for your sake. Through him you believe in God, who raised him from the dead and glorified him, and so your faith and hope are in God.

—1 PETER 1:3, 6–7, 20–21

One of the most unique years of ministry for me was a year when the church I was pastoring unexpectedly received three separate estate gifts. There was a great deal of deferred maintenance that needed to be tended to on the building, but the church simply didn't have the resources to address the projects immediately. That year, the three estate gifts equaled almost exactly what we lacked to address the needs. What made the gifts especially unique was that one of the three was completely unexpected. A couple that had been gone from the church for many years, and whom few remembered, had chosen to leave the church in their will. I have often wondered what their children thought when they discovered that a church their parents had not attended in decades had been included in their family inheritance.

Peter's first epistle is addressed to "exiles" in the world (v. 1)—people who, like their ancestors in faith, have little to claim as their own. However, Peter is convinced that they do still have an incredible inheritance to claim, one that is so valuable that it can never perish, spoil, or fade (v. 4). But what does Peter think we inherit? He lists a handful of things in this text, including both trials and salvation. However, the primary inheritance God's children receive is *a new birth into a living hope through the resurrection of Jesus Christ from the dead.*

One of the most important theological truths for the apostles is the reality of Christ's resurrection. This is very different than Jesus simply coming back from the dead. Don't get me wrong—coming back from the dead is pretty amazing. If I were officiating a funeral and the body sat up and came back to life, the video would go viral! There are people in Scripture who came back from the dead. Elijah raised the widow's son. Jesus brought both Jairus's daughter and Lazarus back to life. However, each of these people died again later from some other cause. They *came back* from the dead—but only Jesus *resurrected* from the dead. Death no longer has dominion over him. This is important for Peter and the other apostolic writers because, as good first-century Jews, they believed that the eschaton—the end of time—would include the resurrection of the dead, God's judgment, and the ushering in of the new creation. Therefore, when Jesus resurrected from the dead, the end (the eschaton), including the new creation, was no longer just waiting at the end of history. It has, in Christ, now broken into the middle of history.

For the early church, when a believer was baptized, the old life was put to death and a new birth into the new creation was enacted.

This is the living hope of the faithful. In Advent, God's people celebrate a reality lived throughout the year. The old broken, violent, rebellious creation is gone, and the new reconciled-to-God world has come and is coming in its fullness. This is the hope that sustains us through the pain of *all kinds of trials* that continue to happen. And this is the hope that leads us to "the end result of your faith, the salvation of your souls" (v. 9).

It is appropriate that this first week of Advent ends with the concept of a living hope. For the hope that is formed in God's people at Advent is not a distant hope but one that is already breaking in as the earth receives her King today and allows him to begin making all things new.

BLESSING FOR THE DAY

Blessed are those whose help is the God of Jacob, whose hope is in the LORD their God. He is the Maker of heaven and earth, the sea, and everything in them—he remains faithful forever.

—PSALM 146:5–6

QUESTIONS FOR REFLECTION

1. What part of the old creation do you need to let go of so you can receive the new creation God has for you?

   _____

   _____

2. Where do you see the new creation at work in your life, in the life of your church, or in the life of your family or community?

   _____

   _____

A RESPONSIVE READING FOR ADVENT HOPE

Reader(s): This first week of Advent is a celebration of hope. God's people are neither optimistic nor pessimistic about the future.

ALL: We are prisoners of hope.

Reader(s): God's people do not put their hope in possessions, in rulers, or in systems and structures.

ALL: Our hope is in the Lord.

Reader(s): God's people learn to be patient in suffering because they know that suffering produces endurance and that endurance produces character.

ALL: And character produces hope, and hope does not disappoint us.

Reader(s): Give thanks to God always because of the grace that has been given to us in Christ Jesus.

ALL: Through him we have become rich in hope.

Reader(s): We are not missing any spiritual gift while we wait for our Lord Jesus Christ to be revealed.

ALL: Our hope is in the Lord. Let earth receive her King.

A FINAL PRAYER FOR ADVENT HOPE

Almighty God, you have invited us to be saved in hope, to wait in hope, and to hope in the hope of your glory. Our hope is that your promise of a new creation is true. Our hope is that in the same way your Son, Jesus Christ, was given new life, the groaning creation will also truly live again in all the ways you intended it to thrive. Our hope is that Christ will reign. Our hope is that the lion will lie down with the lamb. Our hope is that all things will be made new. Forgive us for our inability to live in hope. We too often settle for despair. We build systems of assured destruction and call it peace. We create a culture of sensual self-centeredness and call it love. We chase after conspicuous consumption and call it life. May hope give us a holy discontentment with the world as it is. As we live lives of holy discontent, teach us patient endurance. And as we endure, produce in us a character that reflects your coming kingdom. And may that character be rooted in the hope we have in you. For that hope—the hope of your new life—never disappoints. Amen.

The followers of Jesus have been called to peace. When he called them they found their peace, for he is their peace. But now they are told that they must not only have peace but make it. And to that end they renounce all violence and tumult. In the cause of Christ nothing is to be gained by such methods. His kingdom is one of peace, and the mutual greeting of his flock is a greeting of peace. His disciples keep the peace by choosing to endure suffering themselves rather than inflict it on others. They renounce all self-assertion, and quietly suffer in the face of hatred and wrong. In so doing they overcome evil with good, and establish the peace of God in the midst of a world of war and hate.

—DIETRICH BONHOEFFER,
The Cost of Discipleship

PEACE

Second Sunday of Advent
December 6, 2020

SCRIPTURE READINGS

PSALM 85; ISAIAH 40:1–11; MARK 1:1–8;
2 PETER 3:8–15

But do not forget this one thing, dear friends: With the Lord a day is like a thousand years, and a thousand years are like a day. The Lord is not slow in keeping his promise, as some understand slowness. Instead he is patient with you, not wanting anyone to perish, but everyone to come to repentance.

So then, dear friends, since you are looking forward to this, make every effort to be found spotless, blameless and at peace with him.

—2 PETER 3:8–9, 14

The beauty (and challenge) of Advent is to live faithfully in the reality of the new creation, while still waiting for it to come in its fullness. What God's people relearn each Advent is how to live in between two times: the time of the old creation and the in-breaking of the new.

My new-creation hero in the Bible is Stephen. In Acts 6 and 7, Stephen is accused of blasphemy and brought before the Sanhedrin to face charges. His defense of himself comes in the form of a direct and convicting sermon (my favorite kind). The sermon, however, does not go well (the last straw is probably 7:51, when he calls the religious leaders stiff-necked and uncircumcised). In response, the Sanhedrin drags him out of the city so they can stone him to death.

Here the story gets theologically fascinating. Luke writes, "But Stephen, full of the Holy Spirit, looked up to heaven and saw the glory of God, and Jesus standing at the right hand of God. 'Look,' he said, 'I see heaven open and the Son of Man standing at the right hand of God'" (vv. 55–56). This is an odd vision indeed, but it is also filled with significance. What Stephen sees and describes is essentially the coming of God's kingdom. The followers of Jesus are not simply waiting for him to be at the right hand of the Father. According to Stephen's vision, Jesus is already exalted to the ultimate place of authority.

Stephen saw the reality of the kingdom. He urged those preparing to kill him to look and see it as well. Instead, they covered their ears and refused to look. In response, Stephen knelt down and prayed a prayer of forgiveness (one quite similar to the prayer Jesus prayed on the cross) upon his enemies. Each time I come to this text, I wonder, *what does it take for Stephen to respond to Saul and the angry mob with such grace and peace?* I believe the answer is that God's Spirit gave him the ability to see—and therefore live within—the kingdom reign of Christ. Once we understand that, our interpretation of this event shifts a bit. We certainly still feel pity for Stephen. Stoning is not a good way to die. However, our deepest pity is reserved for Saul and the others who are unable to see that we no longer live in a world where we have to throw rocks at one another.

Similarly, the text from 2 Peter invites believers to live in ways that "look forward to the day of God and speed its coming" (3:12). That doesn't mean our actions may shorten God's redemptive timeline. As Peter implies earlier, the delay in the coming fullness of the kingdom is due to God's patience, *not wanting anyone to perish.* It does, however, mean that we live "looking forward" toward the goal of the new creation. For Peter, that means living in the holiness, blamelessness, and peacefulness of the new creation.

In this second week of Advent, we are invited to practice life under the reign of the Prince of Peace. Like Stephen, and the Christian community receiving Peter's letter, we are invited to live as reflections of Christ's peaceable kingdom. In the New Testament, the word for "martyr" is also translated as "witness." In his peacemaking death, Stephen is not just a martyr but also a witness to the kingdom that even the religious too often fail to see. I am convinced that Saul (or Paul)'s conversion did not begin on the road to Damascus but in Acts 8:1, when he saw in Stephen a peacefulness with God and with others that he did not understand. May the world today witness the reign of the Prince of Peace in his Advent people.

BLESSING FOR THE DAY

Surely his salvation is near those who fear him, that his glory may dwell in our land. Love and faithfulness meet together; righteousness and peace kiss each other.

—PSALM 85:9–10

HYMN FOR THE WEEK

And methinks when I rise to that city of peace
Where the Author of peace I shall see,
That one strain of the song which the ransomed will sing
In that heavenly kingdom shall be:
Peace, peace! Wonderful peace,
Coming down from the Father above,
Sweep over my spirit forever, I pray,
In fathomless billows of love.

QUESTIONS FOR DISCUSSION OR REFLECTION

1. As you look around, both far and near, where are the places you see crying out for peace?

_____

_____

_____

_____

2. What are the primary obstacles to your experiencing peace right now?

_____

_____

_____

_____

3. Who are the Stephens in your life—the people who live as present reflections of Christ's kingdom yet to come in its fullness?

_____

_____

_____

_____

OF HIS PEACE THERE WILL BE NO END

MONDAY, DECEMBER 7, 2020

SCRIPTURE READING

ISAIAH 9:2–7

The people walking in darkness have seen a great light; on those living in the land of deep darkness a light has dawned.

For to us a child is born, to us a son is given, and the government will be on his shoulders. And he will be called Wonderful Counselor, Mighty God, Everlasting Father, Prince of Peace. Of the greatness of his government and peace there will be no end.

ISAIAH 9:2, 6–7a

Political events have the power to divide entire nations, especially when it comes to transitions of power or regime changes. The year 716 BCE was not a good year in Jerusalem. Judah, constantly living under threat of the Assyrian empire, was at a low point politically. The economy wasn't much better. Rather than trusting God, King Ahaz melted down and gave away the nation's most valuable assets in a mafia-style exchange with the king of Assyria for the promise of protection. Spiritual life was also at a low point, having been led by another failed king into fear and idolatry. Mercifully for the people, Ahaz couldn't live forever. After his death, his twenty-four-year-old son Hezekiah replaced him. My guess is that expectations among the Judeans were low and that a great deal of division existed among the people about the prospects of Jerusalem's future.

One might imagine the great prophet Isaiah was invited to bring a few words of wisdom and blessing at Hezekiah's inauguration ceremony. Rather than simply speaking some tactful civil words, Isaiah proclaims a divine renaissance. This new leader will bring light into darkness. The people—all the people—should rejoice as though a great harvest has come and made everyone prosperous. They should rejoice as though a long and deadly war has come to a close. Hezekiah's reign will be the salvation of Jerusalem. All the slogans on his political buttons and bumper stickers will be proven true. Hezekiah will be known throughout Judah's history as a wonderful counselor, as a divinely empowered king, as a loving parent to his citizens, and—most importantly—as the source of an extended period of peace.

Seven centuries later, the period we now think of as the turning of times from BCE to CE was not a very good year in Jerusalem either. It was a time of heavy taxation, aches of exile, and failed revolutions. Like Assyria in the days of Ahaz, Rome pushed the people of God around. These were days of refugee crowds, desperate poverty, debilitating disease, and political unrest. In those dark days, the Gospel writer Matthew recognized that something had changed. He found on the shelf the prophet Isaiah's famous inauguration speech and recontextualized it for another new king. "The people living in darkness have seen a great light; on those living in the land of the shadow of death a light has dawned" (Matthew 4:16). His readers knew the rest of the speech. This new king is a Wonderful Counselor, the Mighty God, the Everlasting Father, the Prince of Peace.

The year 2020 CE is no less turbulent, violent, or divided than 716 BCE or 1 CE. No matter how our political events turn out, in whatever nation we live, the hope of God's people for life, for unity, and for peace remains in the Son born to us who rules like a counselor and who knows our name and our need. He is the very presence of God, able to redeem all things. And, like parents who love their children completely, he is the source of a final and complete peace.

BLESSING FOR THE DAY

The LORD bless you and keep you; the LORD make his face shine on you and be gracious to you; the LORD turn his face toward you and give you peace.

—NUMBERS 6:24–26

QUESTIONS FOR REFLECTION

1. Of the four qualities articulated by Isaiah—counselor, divine presence, loving parent, establisher of peace—which do you most need God to be for you today?

   _____

   _____

   _____

   _____

2. How can God's people (the church), as the unique dwelling place of God's Spirit, embody those four qualities in and for a divided world?

   _____

   _____

   _____

   _____

THOSE WHO PROCLAIM PEACE

TUESDAY, DECEMBER 8, 2020

SCRIPTURE READING

ISAIAH 52:7–10

How beautiful on the mountains are the feet of those who bring good news, who proclaim peace, who bring good tidings, who proclaim salvation, who say to Zion, "Your God reigns!"

The LORD will lay bare his holy arm in the sight of all the nations, and all the ends of the earth will see the salvation of our God.

—ISAIAH 52:7, 10

Several years ago, on a family cruise to Alaska, we spent an evening being entertained by a singer who performed several folk songs from the Yukon Territory. My kids' favorite song of the evening was about the CSS *Shenandoah*, a Confederate war ship that, during the U.S. Civil War, sailed up from Mexico, along the west coast, to the Gulf of Alaska, where it sank several Union whalers and other ships bringing oil and gold to the Northern forces. The crazy part of the story—and the song—was that nearly four months after the Civil War had ended, the *Shenandoah* kept sinking ships because the news had not yet reached the ship's commander and crew that the war was over. It is an interesting piece of American history trivia that the last shot of the Civil War was fired by the *Shenandoah* nearly a hundred days after the war had ended.

The idea of such slow-traveling vital information was not only amusing but also unimaginable for my smartphone-carrying children. It is hard for those of us immersed in a world of instant information to remember that, for most of human history, months and even years could go by before people knew vital political news. Information only moved as fast as the person bringing it.

No wonder the prophet Isaiah proclaims the beauty of the feet of the messenger running across the mountains and proclaiming the end of exile to Judeans scattered across Babylon. The message is received with joy because it is the good news of salvation, redemption, and, in particular, peace. Years of exile and conflict have ended in the restoration of God's peace.

Like the CSS *Shenandoah*, the world today continues to fight a war that is over. In Christ Jesus, peace was made between God and humankind, thus opening the door for peace to be made between brothers, sisters, and even enemies. The war is over. Unfortunately, unnecessary shots continue to be fired. The world needs the beautiful feet of messengers carrying to every corner of creation the good news of peace in Christ Jesus. To whom can you bring the good tidings of peace today?

BLESSING FOR THE DAY

The LORD sits enthroned over the flood; the LORD is enthroned as King forever. The LORD gives strength to his people; the LORD blesses his people with peace.

—PSALM 29:10–11

QUESTIONS FOR REFLECTION

1. Who was the first person to bring you the good news of Christ's peace? Give God thanks for them today.

   _____

   _____

   _____

   _____

2. Whom do you know who needs to hear the good news that peace is possible in and through Christ? How could you be the beautiful feet of peace for them today?

   _____

   _____

   _____

   _____

   _____

MY PEACE
I GIVE YOU

SCRIPTURE READING

JOHN 14:25–31

Peace I leave with you; my peace I give you. I do not give to
you as the world gives. Do not let your hearts be troubled and
do not be afraid.

—JOHN 14:27

At the end of a protracted war, there is finally a treaty or agree-
ment to establish peace. However, it isn't really peace, is it? We call
it peace, but it is really just one side deciding it has had enough
loss, bloodshed, and devastation. It is a peace formed through the
conquest of another.

Enemy nations may also establish peace by increasing their
strength to such a degree that others are afraid to attack. This too
we call peace, but it is actually just mutually assured destruction.
It is a peace formed through the fear of death.

This, to quote Jesus, is too often the way "the world gives" peace. It is
not true peace. It is the temporary absence of open conflict. It does
not bring unity. Instead, it further alienates. It does not offer forgiveness. Instead, it internalizes past wrongs. It does not invite reconciliation. Instead, it waits for a sign of weakness that may be exploited.

In his well-known book *Peace Child*, missionary Don Richardson
describes his work among the Sawi people of New Guinea. After

living among them for some time and beginning to tell the stories of the Bible, he was shocked to discover their interest in knowing more about Judas as a hero. As a tribe constantly dealing with cycles of violence and treachery, they were very interested in knowing more about this one who was able to befriend and then betray Jesus. (By the way, if you come to the end of sharing the gospel story with someone, and they come away from it seeing Judas as the hero, something is wrong.)

The Richardsons soon learned about a tradition practiced among some of the warring tribes. In order to end the violence, each village would present their enemy tribe with an infant child to care for. As long as this foreign child lived and was cared for by the other tribe, this "peace child" became the source of peace. In this practice, Richardson found the metaphor he needed to share the good news of Jesus. Christ is like the peace child offered by the Sawi to their enemies. In giving his Son to the world, God made peace with his rebellious creatures.

However, Christ is also *unlike* the peace child. As John states in today's text, Jesus does not bring peace the way the world does. The world can only imagine a peace that is rooted in fear and threat. On the cross, Jesus took on the sin and violence of humankind and responded not with threat but with love and grace. In this way, Jesus offered peace with God and with one another, not through more threat but through reconciliation and forgiveness. This is the peace—the true peace—the church not only celebrates at Advent, but also embodies as we look forward to the lion and lamb learning to live with one another in peace.

BLESSING FOR THE DAY

Pray for the peace of Jerusalem: "May those who love you be secure. May there be peace within your walls and security within your citadels." For the sake of my family and friends, I will say, "Peace be within you."

—PSALM 122:6–8

QUESTIONS FOR REFLECTION

1. How does the world offer peace? What are the limitations and problems with that kind of peace?

   _____

   _____

   _____

   _____

2. How is the peace of Jesus different than that offered by the world? What would it look like to offer one another that kind of peace?

   _____

   _____

   _____

   _____

THUS MAKING PEACE

THURSDAY, DECEMBER 10, 2020

SCRIPTURE READING

EPHESIANS 2:14–17

For he himself is our peace, who has made the two groups one and has destroyed the barrier, the dividing wall of hostility, by setting aside in his flesh the law with its commands and regulations. His purpose was to create in himself one new humanity out of the two, thus making peace, and in one body to reconcile both of them to God through the cross, by which he put to death their hostility. He came and preached peace to you who were far away and peace to those who were near.

—EPHESIANS 2:14–17

By the time a reader gets to the end of the eleventh chapter of Genesis they get a picture of a world that is quite a mess. At the conclusion of the story of the Tower of Babel, Scripture has painted a picture of a world filled with sin, violence, confusion, and division. It is anything but a place of peace.

At the end of the second chapter of Acts—the story of Pentecost—a different picture emerges. The world is still very diverse. It is filled with "Parthians, Medes and Elamites; residents of Mesopotamia, Judea and Cappadocia, Pontus and Asia, Phrygia and Pamphylia, Egypt and the parts of Libya near Cyrene; visitors from Rome (both Jews and converts to Judaism); Cretans and Arabs" (Acts 2:9–11a). It is as though Luke wants readers to picture every tribe and ethnicity under heaven gathered together in Jerusalem that day. When the Spirit of the Lord is poured out upon those gathered, their diversity and uniqueness are not taken away; however, in and through the power of the Holy Spirit, they find unity.

This unity in the Spirit of Jesus animates the theology behind Paul's letter to the Ephesians. In Christ, all of the dividing walls between people have been brought down. In this new body—the church—peace is being proclaimed to those *who were far away and peace to those who were near.* As I read Paul's epistles, I'm struck by the idea that Paul could not imagine making "peace" between people as different as Jews and gentiles by forming one congregation for Jewish Christians and another for gentile Christians. No way! They had to learn to live together in peace—not by becoming all alike but by learning to live in the unity of Christ's spirit despite their differences. In this way, they not only know but also *embody* the peace of the new creation to the world.

I am sometimes suspicious of churches where the majority of people are the same ethnicity, of a similar generation, the same social status, and/or even aligned politically. It does not take the work of the Holy Spirit to get a group of people together who share the same demographics. For the apostle Paul, the church is a different body (a *new humanity*) that is united in ways the world simply does not understand. Unity in the midst of our diversity is the sign of the Spirit's presence and the church's witness of peace to a deeply divided world.

As Reuben Welch wrote so beautifully a number of years ago now, "No matter how long it takes us, we've got to go together. Because that's how it is in the body of Christ. It's all of us in love, in care, in support, in mutuality—we really do need each other."

BLESSING FOR THE DAY

May the God of hope fill you with all joy and peace as you trust in him, so that you may overflow with hope by the power of the Holy Spirit.

—ROMANS 15:13

QUESTIONS FOR REFLECTION

1. What are the forces that keep the world divided? How are those forces of division pictured in the first eleven chapters of Genesis?

_____

_____

_____

_____

2. What would it look like for the world to live not in uniformity but in unity?

_____

_____

_____

_____

3. How can the church practice the life of unity in the Spirit by bringing together those who are too often divided?

_____

_____

_____

_____

THE GOD
OF PEACE

FRIDAY, DECEMBER 11, 2020

SCRIPTURE READING

PHILIPPIANS 4:4–9

Rejoice in the Lord always. I will say it again: Rejoice! Let
your gentleness be evident to all. The Lord is near. Do not be
anxious about anything, but in every situation, by prayer and
petition, with thanksgiving, present your requests to God.
And the peace of God, which transcends all understanding,
will guard your hearts and your minds in Christ Jesus.
Finally, brothers and sisters, whatever is true, whatever
is noble, whatever is right, whatever is pure, whatever is
lovely, whatever is admirable—if anything is excellent or
praiseworthy—think about such things. Whatever you have
learned or received or heard from me, or seen in me—put it
into practice. And the God of peace will be with you.

—PHILIPPIANS 4:4–9

Philippians 4:4–9 is a deeply loved passage of Scripture. Verse 6
was one of the first verses I memorized as a child. In kindergarten,
I was the last person in the class to learn how to skip. The teachers
and other students had been trying for several days to help me
figure out what I just couldn't seem to get my feet to accomplish.
A friend was staying with our family at the time. She asked me if I
had prayed about it and asked God to help me learn to skip. I was
only five, but already this seemed to me like too minor a problem
to take to the Creator of the universe. She taught me to memorize

Paul's encouraging command to the Philippian church. Sure enough, after sincere prayer, the next day my feet finally figured out how to skip. Thanks be to God.

What I love most about Paul's stirring instructions to rejoice, pray, think about the excellent and the praiseworthy—and then receive peace—is that they are given in the midst of a broken and difficult life situation. If the reader backs up just a few verses, they find Paul pleading with two women, Euodia and Syntyche, to end their disagreement. (An argument that was intense enough to have come to the attention of the apostle? Yikes!) This beloved text from Philippians 4 is spoken directly into a church fight.

Yesterday's reflection concentrated on the beauty of God's people when the Spirit brings unity. I can think of many times in my life when I have experienced a beauty that can only be described as the in-breaking of a new creation among the people Christ calls his church. However, I can also think (and give you a detailed list if you would like one) of the many deep, painful, and hurtful conflicts that I have not only witnessed but also, unfortunately, found myself directly involved. Like Jesus, the body of Christ bears many scars—not just as signs of healing but also as reminders of how often we hurt and do damage to one another. Into the reality of interpersonal, disciple-to-disciple conflict, Paul encourages not just Euodia and Syntyche but also the whole community to lean into the following practices.

Rejoice in the Lord. Stop focusing on what was lost or taken away in conflict. Rather, give attention to the blessings of God often given through the other.

Pray. Invite the nearness and gentleness of God to become evident in the circumstances.

Focus on the praiseworthy. It is too easy in conflict for the negative to take up all the space in our hearts. Rather than giving sole voice to that which brings brokenness, focus instead on that which is good and brings healing.

Practice and receive peace. I love the image in the text that God's peace might stand guard over our hearts and minds. Conflict, even in the body of Christ, is inevitable. Where two or three are gathered together, eventually there will be disagreement. However, it is also there that Christ dwells in our midst, helping us to make peace and to guard our hearts and minds from turning conflict into division.

BLESSING FOR THE DAY

Let the peace of Christ rule in your hearts, since as members of one body you were called to peace. And be thankful.

—COLOSSIANS 3:15

QUESTIONS FOR REFLECTION

1. Where are the scars and wounds of conflict causing you pain?

    _____

    _____

    _____

    _____

2. How might this text invite you to respond today?

    _____

    _____

    _____

    _____

3. List three of the most praiseworthy things that come to mind. Rejoice in them. Give thanks for them. Center your mind on them today.

    _____

    _____

    _____

    _____

SOW IN PEACE

SATURDAY, DECEMBER 12, 2020

SCRIPTURE READING

JAMES 3:17–18

But the wisdom that comes from heaven is first of all pure; then peace-loving, considerate, submissive, full of mercy and good fruit, impartial and sincere. Peacemakers who sow in peace reap a harvest of righteousness.

—JAMES 3:17–18

There is a kind of "wisdom" that is certainly not new to this present age; instead it shows up in a number of different spheres in the culture. It is a kind of wisdom that believes one should win at all costs. There is certainly a prevalent model of leadership in the culture that attempts to "win" by never showing weakness, refusing to apologize (even if clearly in the wrong), name-calling one's enemies, and demonizing anyone considered to be part of the opposition. It's not unusual these days to even hear Christian leaders praise people in fields as diverse as sports, business, and politics for living out this no-holds-barred kind of wisdom.

The epistle of James is not unfamiliar with this way of thinking. Beginning in chapter 3, James is critical of all the ways the tongue can be used to tell lies, tear down others, brag, boast, and exacerbate conflict. One can almost picture those first-century leaders who are the likely targets of James's criticism. Look out for those skilled in rhetoric and using it not for the common good but for their own selfish benefit. Such "wisdom," says James, "does not come down from heaven but is earthly, unspiritual, demonic" (3:15).

There is, however, another kind of wisdom for James. This kind of wisdom *is first of all pure; then peace-loving, considerate, submissive, full of mercy and good fruit, impartial and sincere.* This is the kind of wisdom—which philosophers of the day and early Christian writers often called *logos*—that Jesus embodied in the incarnation. This kind of life may seem foolish rather than wise from the perspective of those who live from the world's wisdom. However, those who keep planting the peaceful seeds of God's wisdom will be vindicated when the harvest of righteousness is raised up.

I suppose that is a good place to conclude the emphasis on peace in this second week of Advent. James invites us to wonder what kind of wisdom we are sowing in the world. Are we sowing the seeds of continued division and conflict embodied in the old creation and passing away with the coming of Christ? Or are we sowing the seeds of peace that are consistent with the new creation, a peace that operates as a foretaste of the Lord's coming harvest of peace? This is not an easy calling. It takes living with a kind of patience and wisdom we don't have much of by our own strength. Perhaps that is why, in his opening chapter, James invites those lacking this kind of wisdom to ask God, "who gives generously to all without finding fault" (v. 5). It is the wisdom of the new creation. It is the wisdom of the Prince of Peace. Let earth receive her King of peace.

BLESSING FOR THE DAY

May God himself, the God of peace, sanctify you through and through. May your whole spirit, soul and body be kept blameless at the coming of our Lord Jesus Christ. The one who calls you is faithful, and he will do it.

—1 THESSALONIANS 5:23–24

QUESTIONS FOR REFLECTION

1. Where do you see the world's wisdom at work today? How are you tempted to live into that kind of life?

    _____

    _____

    _____

    _____

2. What does it look like to sow the seeds of God's wisdom in the world? Why does that take faith?

    _____

    _____

    _____

    _____

3. Where do you need God to give you his kind of wisdom today? Ask for that wisdom and trust God to give it to you.

    _____

    _____

    _____

    _____

A RESPONSIVE READING FOR ADVENT PEACE

Reader(s): The second week of Advent is a prayer for peace. In a world deeply divided . . .

ALL: Christ is our peace. He breaks down every dividing wall.

Reader(s): In a world filled with hostility and hatred . . .

ALL: Christ is our peace. He teaches us to love our enemies.

Reader(s): In a world of war, where violence never ends . . .

ALL: Christ is our peace. He invites us to take up our cross and follow him.

Reader(s): A shoot will grow up from the stump of Jesse; a branch will sprout from his roots.

ALL: The Lord's spirit will rest upon him, a spirit of wisdom and understanding.

Reader(s): Righteousness will be the belt around his hips, and faithfulness the belt around his waist.

ALL: The wolf will live with the lamb, and the leopard will lie down with the young goat; and a little child will lead them.

Reader(s): They won't harm or destroy anywhere on my holy mountain.

ALL: The earth will surely be filled with the knowledge of the Lord, just as the water covers the sea. Let earth receive her King!

A FINAL PRAYER FOR ADVENT PEACE

Almighty God, you have invited us to live at peace with you, to live in peace with one another, to make peace in a divided world. We confess how hard it is for us to imagine the lion and the lamb lying down together. That kind of peace is beyond anything we have ever experienced. Teach us to live in faith and not fear. Teach us how to witness to a new creation. Teach us how to make peace. Forgive us for our inability to live in peace. We don't want to simply live in fear of one another. We invite the Prince of Peace to come. Let his peace begin in us. Amen.

Joy . . . is here a technical term and must be sharply distinguished both from Happiness and from Pleasure. Joy has indeed one characteristic . . . the fact that anyone who has experienced it will want it again . . . I doubt whether anyone who has tasted it would ever, if both were in his power, exchange it for all the pleasures in the world. But then Joy is never in our power and pleasure often is.

—C. S. LEWIS,
Surprised by Joy

JOY

Third Sunday of Advent
December 13, 2020

SCRIPTURE READINGS

PSALM 126; **ISAIAH 61:1–4, 8–11;** JOHN 1:6–8, 19–28;
1 THESSALONIANS 5:16–24

The Spirit of the Sovereign LORD is on me, because the LORD
has anointed me to proclaim good news to the poor. He has
sent me to bind up the brokenhearted, to proclaim freedom
for the captives and release from darkness for the prisoners, to
proclaim the year of the LORD's favor and the day of vengeance
of our God, to comfort all who mourn, and provide for those
who grieve in Zion—to bestow on them a crown of beauty
instead of ashes, the oil of joy instead of mourning, and a
garment of praise instead of a spirit of despair. They will be
called oaks of righteousness, a planting of the LORD for the
display of his splendor.

I delight greatly in the LORD; my soul rejoices in my God. For
he has clothed me with garments of salvation and arrayed
me in a robe of his righteousness, as a bridegroom adorns
his head like a priest, and as a bride adorns herself with
her jewels. For as the soil makes the sprout come up and a
garden causes seeds to grow, so the Sovereign LORD will make
righteousness and praise spring up before all nations.

—ISAIAH 61:1–3, 10–11

The narrative of Israel's deliverance from Pharaoh is not just a story about how God got his people out of Egypt. It is also a story about how God got Egypt out of them. The forty years in the wilderness formed (actually, *re-formed*) Israel into a people who would reflect God's way, God's purposes, and God's new creation life to the world. On Mount Sinai Moses was given the Torah—the law that, when lived out by God's people, would be the embodiment of a redeemed life in right connection to God and others.

The Torah covers every aspect of life, even economics. There are several economic laws, or codes, in the Torah (they often are referred to as "Levitical codes"), but there are four that are primary.

The first is tithing. Ten percent of everything raised or made was taken to the storehouses for care of the priests and the poor in the community. Keeping Sabbath and observing the sabbatical year is the second key code. Every seven days the people rested, and every seventh year they let everything, including the land and animals, rest in God's care. The third code is gleaning. The Israelites were not to harvest the edges of their fields, and when they got to the corners, they left a wide swath of grain. Through gleaning, God's people were always prepared for the needs of the alien, the sojourner, or the refugee in their midst.

The last code is the most difficult, and it relates to Isaiah 61. Leviticus 25 outlines the law of Jubilee. After seven cycles of sabbatical years (forty-nine years) another year (the fiftieth) was to become a complete resetting of the economic system. On the first day of the fiftieth year, the trumpets (the *jubals*) were to be sounded, and all debts were to be forgiven, all prisoners released, and everyone allowed to return to their ancestral land. The Year of Jubilee was meant to be a time for grace to flow and for everyone to get a do-over.

As far as we know, Israel enacted the first three codes—tithing, Sabbath/sabbatical, and gleaning—faithfully. Yet they failed to ever proclaim the Year of Jubilee (the year of the Lord's favor). It is this year of transforming grace that the prophet proclaims in Isaiah chapter 61. Even though Israel and Judah failed to proclaim the great renewal of Jubilee for one another, God—by delivering the people out of Babylon—proclaimed a new beginning for them. Ironically, through the eyes of the prophet, the rubble of Jerusalem is not a cause for despair but a source of great joy. It is the wiping clean of the past, and the opportunity, with God's help, for Jerusalem to begin anew. What the people saw as a disaster, God viewed as a new start.

The prophet proclaims three "insteads" over them. Because of God's faithfulness the people would receive a crown of joy instead of ashes, gladness instead of mourning, and praise instead of a spirit of despair. He also announces what they would now become because of the gracious activity of God. They will be oaks of righteousness. They will rebuild the ancient ruins. They will renew the ruined cities.

In Advent, where the world despairs in darkness, God's people rejoice in the possibility for light to break in. Where the world lives mired in sin, God's people rejoice in the potential of transforming and sanctifying grace. Where the world feels trapped in evil, God's people anticipate the world-turning power of good. And where the world anguishes over death, God's people rejoice in the coming of Christ's resurrection life.

BLESSING FOR THE DAY

But let all who take refuge in you be glad; let them ever sing for joy. Spread your protection over them, that those who love your name may rejoice in you.

—PSALM 5:11

HYMN FOR THE WEEK

Joyful, joyful, we adore thee,
God of glory, Lord of love;
Hearts unfold like flowers before thee,
Opening to the sun above.
Melt the clouds of sin and sadness;
Drive the dark of doubt away;
Giver of immortal gladness,
Fill us with the light of day!

QUESTIONS FOR DISCUSSION OR REFLECTION

1. In what ways has God proclaimed a Jubilee in your life?

    _____

    _____

    _____

    _____

2. Whom do you know who needs to hear the good news of a new start by God's grace?

    _____

    _____

    _____

    _____

3. What are your greatest sources of joy this season? Give God thanks for them.

    _____

    _____

    _____

    _____

SING FOR JOY
BEFORE THE LORD

MONDAY, DECEMBER 14, 2020

SCRIPTURE READING

1 CHRONICLES 16:27–33

Splendor and majesty are before him; strength and joy are in his dwelling place.

Let the heavens rejoice, let the earth be glad; let them say among the nations, "The LORD reigns!" Let the sea resound, and all that is in it; let the fields be jubilant, and everything in them! Let the trees of the forest sing, let them sing for joy before the LORD, for he comes to judge the earth.

—1 CHRONICLES 16:27, 31–33

There is an old proverb that states: *power corrupts; absolute power corrupts absolutely*. Many of our favorite stories are crafted around the question of what people would do if they were suddenly given all kinds of power. Would they use that power for good? Or would they misuse the power for greed and for themselves? That question should probably be the lens through which we read the story of David and the ark of the covenant, found in 1 Chronicles 15–16 and also 2 Samuel 6.

Although God's people understood that God exists everywhere, they were convinced that the unique and powerful presence of God existed most intensely between the cherubim on the mercy seat of the ark. In these chapters of Chronicles and in 2 Samuel 6, David is trying desperately to bring the ark into his new capital and make it the geographical and symbolic center of the city. Things don't go so well. He tries to speed up the process and get it there on a new cart. That ends in disaster and death (poor Uzzah). Finally, with sacrifices and dancing, the ark arrives in the tabernacle with the joyous sounds of the psalm that is part of today's text as its marching music.

It seems to me that the point of the topsy-turvy David-and-the-ark stories is that God is more than happy to dwell in the center of the life of God's people. However, God's presence is not a force or power to be manipulated. God will not allow his unique presence to be used by David to reinforce his own power. The glory of God may be found between the cherubim, but God will not be controlled. The unique and powerful presence of God can only be received with joy and gladness.

Like the divine presence itself, there is no formula for having or experiencing joy. Joy cannot be controlled, possessed, or held onto with a firm grip. Joy is not the byproduct of having security and living without risk. That was David's initial quest—to have control and live in security. Rather, joy—like God's presence—can only be received with gratitude as one perceives the work of God, even, if not often, in difficult circumstances. We can dance in and receive in openness the joy of the Lord, but we can't constrain it.

I have a friend who, though facing significant physical suffering for the last several years, continues to live with joy. I often ask her how she continues her journey with such joy. Her response is usually simple. "I look for God mysteriously at work each day," she says, "and receive what he has for me and what he is doing in me with joy."

Advent reminds us that we do not control the in-breaking of God. It always comes mysteriously and unexpectedly. However, we can receive the coming of Christ each moment with joy.

BLESSING FOR THE DAY

You make known to me the path of life; you will fill me with joy in your presence, with eternal pleasures at your right hand.

—PSALM 16:11

QUESTIONS FOR REFLECTION

1. In the story of David receiving the ark with joy, his joy is contrasted with the bitterness and barrenness of his wife, Michal, near the end of 2 Samuel 6. Why does she miss out on the joy of the Lord?

2. Are there ways that you sense yourself trying, like David, to control or manipulate the presence of God?

3. Where do you see God at work today? How can you receive God's presence and God's work with joy?

THE JOY OF THE LORD IS YOUR STRENGTH

SCRIPTURE READING

NEHEMIAH 8:7–12

The Levites . . . instructed the people in the Law while the people were standing there. They read from the Book of the Law of God, making it clear and giving the meaning so that the people understood what was being read. Then Nehemiah the governor, Ezra the priest and teacher of the Law, and the Levites who were instructing the people said to them all, "This day is holy to the LORD your God. Do not mourn or weep." For all the people had been weeping as they listened to the words of the Law. Nehemiah said, "Go and enjoy choice food and sweet drinks, and send some to those who have nothing prepared. This day is holy to our Lord. Do not grieve, for the joy of the LORD is your strength." The Levites calmed all the people, saying, "Be still, for this is a holy day. Do not grieve." Then all the people went away to eat and drink, to send portions of food and to celebrate with great joy, because they now understood the words that had been made known to them.

—NEHEMIAH 8:7–12

When I was a student in undergrad, the vice president of my university showed me an aerial map he had made of the campus. On the map he had marked off the part that he envisioned becoming the center of campus, which would require several streets to be blocked off and rerouted as well as a number of buildings added over time. I remember thinking it all sounded a bit crazy and too far out in the distant future to become reality. That vice president later became the university president and worked diligently to see those dreams come to fruition. I graduated and headed off to other places, but I have since returned to the area after thirty years away. Last year the ribbon-cutting and dedication ceremony took place for the last building on that aerial dream map from three decades ago. I stood among other alumni at the ceremony and couldn't help but tear up, thinking about the blessing of dreamers and the faithfulness of God.

As we have been experiencing, many of the texts during Advent come out of the time of exile. The books Ezra and Nehemiah narrate the spiritual and physical rebuilding project that was post-exilic Jerusalem. In today's text there is a dedication ceremony of sorts going on. The temple has been rebuilt. The walls of Jerusalem were close to being complete. The people told Ezra to bring the book of the Law and stand on a newly built platform and read it aloud to all who were gathered. The people are described as eager, attentive, and worshipful.

As Ezra read the Torah, the people stood, clapped, and shouted. It is said that the shouts could be heard from miles away. The people also wept. It is likely that, as they heard the stories of God's deliverance of Israel from the first exile, they were moved to tears at the faithfulness of God to deliver them from their second exile. They were also likely reminded of their sin and brokenness that had led them back into exile in the first place.

Although weeping—especially in repentance or in gratitude—is not inappropriate as a response, Nehemiah sensed that this occasion of renewal and dedication called for another response: joy. Nehemiah sent the people home to eat good food and drink sweet wine with thanksgiving. As they rejoiced and partied, they were to include their neighbors so the entire community could join the celebration. Weeping and repentance have their place, but *the joy of the* LORD *is your strength*.

There are at least twelve festivals celebrated in the Old Testament, and almost every one of them lasts for a week or more! There is a time to weep. There is a time to make plans. There is a time to work and rebuild. However, there is also a time for celebration and joy, acknowledging all that God's grace has done and is bringing to completion.

BLESSING FOR THE DAY

The LORD is my strength and my shield; my heart trusts in him, and he helps me. My heart leaps for joy, and with my song I praise him.

—PSALM 28:7

QUESTIONS FOR REFLECTION

1. If you could take an aerial photograph of your life, what are the places of change you could point out where you can see that God's hand was at work?

   _____

   _____

2. Where do you see God at work next?

   _____

   _____

3. Celebrations for God's people are never simply private. When God's people rejoice, the neighbors get included too. Whom can you invite into the joy of the Lord today?

   _____

   _____

SHOUT FOR JOY

WEDNESDAY, DECEMBER 16, 2020

SCRIPTURE READING

PSALM 100

Shout for joy to the LORD, all the earth. Worship the LORD with gladness; come before him with joyful songs. Know that the LORD is God. It is he who made us, and we are his; we are his people, the sheep of his pasture. Enter his gates with thanksgiving and his courts with praise; give thanks to him and praise his name. For the LORD is good and his love endures forever; his faithfulness continues through all generations.

—PSALM 100

We have a delightful goldendoodle named Henley. She loves to go out her doggy door and play in the backyard. Our home has a beautiful view of water and mountains, and she likes to sit out there like Simba in *The Lion King*—overlooking all that the light touches as though it is her domain. She chases birds and squirrels and barks at the Labrador two doors down. We have a large picture window where I often sit, drink coffee, read, and get tickled at her playfulness. When I'm ready for her to come in all I have to do is tap a couple of times on the window. She has learned that this is the signal to come and play, come and eat, or come and get in the car for an adventure. Two short taps, and she comes running.

I have grown to love calls to worship at the beginning of a worship service. Sometimes the call to worship is sung. Sometimes it is shouted out. Often it is given in the form of a call and response. The point of the practice is that God's people don't show up for worship each week simply out of habit. They come in response to the voice of God inviting God's people to gather in his presence. The God who delights in us each day as we serve him in the world taps on the glass, if you will, and we run with joy (and wagging tails) to play, to eat, to continue our adventure together with him.

This is the spirit of Psalm 100. It is a call to worship to which God's people joyously respond. As we come to worship, three important truths are affirmed. First, *the LORD is God*. People in the ancient world viewed the world as full of gods, but Israel understood that Yahweh, or Jehovah, alone was God. In another call to worship psalm, Psalm 121, as the people ascend the mountain to the temple, they look around at the mountains and likely at all the "holy places" of the other gods that sit atop them, and ask, "Where does my help come from?" (121:1). The world goes looking for help in all kinds of places, but with our ancient ancestors in faith, we proclaim that our "help comes from the LORD" (121:2).

Secondly, Psalm 100 affirms that *we are his people, the sheep of his pasture*. There is a bit of scandal in the call to worship—because not everyone is responding. In my last ministry assignment, I ran into my neighbor almost every Sunday morning. We both walked out our front doors right around seven o'clock in the morning. I was in my suit or jacket, headed for the church. He was in his robe, coffee in hand, headed to the end of the driveway to pick up his Sunday edition of the newspaper. We always waved and said a few neighborly words. As I drove away, I prayed that at some point my neighbor too might hear the tap on the glass—the voice of God— calling him to come and know that the Lord is God and to know the care of the Lord as a shepherd. In the meantime, there exists the scandal of a particular people—a particular flock—gathering by grace to be formed as a unique people in the world.

Finally, Psalm 100 celebrates that *the LORD is good and his love endures forever*. The invitation to worship is the invitation to be drawn close to the heart and goodness of God. Brent Peterson has beautifully likened both the call to worship and the blessing/sending back into the world (often called the benediction) to a form of divine breathing. In *Created to Worship*, Peterson says, "God breathes (inhales) and gathers in individual Christians to heal, transform, and renew them as the body of Christ to breathe (exhale) them out to continue the ministry of the incarnation that participates in the kingdom of God more fully coming."

During Advent, many of our neighbors may see the sights of the season without hearing the voice of God calling them to rejoice and come worship the newborn King. May we not be so distracted by the season's busyness that we fail to hear the divine invitation to come and worship. Listen for the tap on the glass.

BLESSING FOR THE DAY

You turned my wailing into dancing; you removed my sackcloth and clothed me with joy.

PSALM 30:11

QUESTIONS FOR REFLECTION

1.   Why is it important to sense the call to worship and not simply worship out of discipline or duty?

2.   Which of the affirmations of Psalm 100 speak most meaningfully to you today?

3.   What is scandalous about responding to the call to worship? What is unique about the people who hear that call?

EVERLASTING JOY

SCRIPTURE READING

ISAIAH 35:1–10

The desert and the parched land will be glad; the wilderness will rejoice and blossom. Like the crocus, it will burst into bloom; it will rejoice greatly and shout for joy. The glory of Lebanon will be given to it, the splendor of Carmel and Sharon; they will see the glory of the LORD, the splendor of our God. Strengthen the feeble hands, steady the knees that give way; say to those with fearful hearts, "Be strong, do not fear; your God will come, he will come with vengeance; with divine retribution he will come to save you." Then will the eyes of the blind be opened and the ears of the deaf unstopped. Then will the lame leap like a deer, and the mute tongue shout for joy. Water will gush forth in the wilderness and streams in the desert. The burning sand will become a pool, the thirsty ground bubbling springs. In the haunts where jackals once lay, grass and reeds and papyrus will grow. And a highway will be there; it will be called the Way of Holiness; it will be for those who walk on that Way. The unclean will not journey on it; wicked fools will not go about on it. No lion will be there, nor any ravenous beast; they will not be found there. But only the redeemed will walk there, and those the LORD has rescued will return. They will enter Zion with singing; everlasting joy will crown their heads. Gladness and joy will overtake them, and sorrow and sighing will flee away.

—ISAIAH 35:1–10

We were driving on vacation recently when we encountered a major traffic backup on the highway just a couple of hours from home. Cars were stopped and backed up for a mile or more. People were out sitting on their hoods and talking to their neighboring travelers. The word being passed around from the far-off front, like a highway game of telephone, was that there was a serious, fatal accident up ahead that took up all the lanes on the highway. Because we were miles from a major city, it had taken some time for help to arrive. An investigation was underway, and there would be no cars passing through either direction for at least two hours.

Looking at the map on my phone, I estimated that we could drive back over a hundred miles and cut across, taking a different route home. The problem was that this detour would add at least three or four hours to our travel time. There also appeared to be a dirt road on the map, about a mile back, that looped out into the vast expanse of nothingness beside us, eventually reconnecting to the highway about seven miles up ahead. My guess was that if we took that dirt road, it would bypass the accident, and we could be on our way again.

I drove back about a mile, and sure enough, there was a break in the fence running alongside the highway—a dirt "road" leading into the wilderness. Against the protests of every other family member in the car, I decided to take us on an adventure. The next ten miles took over an hour and were filled with prayer and fear. What road there was had clearly been built for ATVs, *not* family-sized SUVs. We got stuck twice and had to get out and push the car out of holes or off of high places. Three or four times we had to backtrack because the road was so hard to determine and follow. I kept thinking about what I would tell the authorities if they had to come and rescue us or what derogatory stories would be told at my funeral in a few months after they found our bodies in the desert. Thankfully, we got back to the highway eventually, and actually made it home. The car—and my marriage—survived. It took three loops through the car wash and a bit of tire realignment, but all was well.

The text for today imagines God's people having to travel on "roads" in the wilderness. They are on a journey through challenges in life that few, if any, have taken before them. There are no maps and no signs. Isaiah 34 proclaims the kind of judgment and destruction that fall on the nations that attempt this journey by their own strength—they fall and die. But Isaiah 35, today's text, imagines God's people taking this adventure through the wilderness of life with God's Law—the Way of Holiness—as their guide. They don't know what challenges lie ahead on their path through the wilderness, but the prophet promises that God will be with them, turning parched places into gardens and dangerous spots into havens of protection and care. Most importantly, the prophet promises that the people will get to their destination. *They will enter Zion with singing; everlasting joy will crown their heads. Gladness and joy will overtake them, and sorrow and sighing will flee away.*

Life can often feel like a journey through the wilderness without a map. God's promise to God's people is not that the journey will come without challenges (some of them significant) but that God's Word and presence would guide, nurture, care, protect, and ultimately get us safely home with joy.

BLESSING FOR THE DAY

You love righteousness and hate wickedness; therefore God, your God, has set you above your companions by anointing you with the oil of joy.

—PSALM 45:7

QUESTIONS FOR REFLECTION

1. Where are the places that feel most like wilderness for you today?

   _____

   _____

   _____

   _____

2. How has God's Word and God's presence led you through difficult places in the past?

   _____

   _____

   _____

   _____

3. Ask God to make his presence, care, and direction known to you today.

   _____

   _____

   _____

   _____

NO ONE WILL TAKE AWAY YOUR JOY

FRIDAY, DECEMBER 18, 2020

SCRIPTURE READING

JOHN 16:16–24

Very truly I tell you, you will weep and mourn while the world rejoices. You will grieve, but your grief will turn to joy. A woman giving birth to a child has pain because her time has come; but when her baby is born she forgets the anguish because of her joy that a child is born into the world. So with you: Now is your time of grief, but I will see you again and you will rejoice, and no one will take away your joy.

—JOHN 16:20–22

My father is dying. Recently, his oncologists discovered that the aggressive form of cancer he has been battling had returned. They estimate that he has just a handful of months left to live. There are many losses I am already grieving and preparing to grieve at his death. However, the greatest ache in my heart comes from imagining all the future events for which he will not be present. There will be a gap and an empty space in family weddings, births, and holidays without him there to share in the celebrations. I am having a hard time picturing events of significance happening in my life and in my ministry without my dad being there to share in the moment. Many, if not most, of you are also experiencing that sense of sadness and grief because of a missing loved one. The heartwarming seasons of Advent and Christmas can be painful and agonizing for those of us who grieve the absence of family and friends.

It is this sense of grief in absence that Jesus addresses in the text for today. Jesus warns the disciples that a time is coming soon when they will not see him anymore. This one who is so central to their life and identity, so present to them in their journey of discipleship, will be gone. His words here are certainly directed toward the twelve disciples who will not see Jesus after the crucifixion but who *will* see him again after the resurrection. Their weeping at the suffering and death of Jesus will become the source for their rejoicing and celebration when they see the risen Lord again.

It seems, however, that the text is also meant to be read by early Christians (and by us today) as a way of narrating their (and our) experience. The church celebrates the risen Christ, but God's people also experience the bodily absence of the Lord. The church mourns the absence of the physical Savior after his ascension to the Father, but during Advent we anticipate that we will see him again and that *no one will take away our joy*.

The path to the new creation always involves suffering. The metaphor used by Jesus here and also by the apostle Paul in Romans 8 is childbirth. The struggles that disciples face in the seeming absence of the Lord are the birth pangs of the new creation. In the meantime, in the space where the bodily presence of Christ is absent, the presence of the Holy Spirit enters in and continues the reshaping work of Jesus. Three times, in three successive chapters of John's Gospel, Jesus invites the disciples to pray in the expansive hope that "whatever you ask in my name" will be done. He states this promise first in 14:13, then again in 15:16, and once again in the text for today, in 16:23. Of course, the phrase "in my name" gives direction and motivation to the "whatever" disciples are invited to pray for. To catch the right emphasis, we could translate "in my name" into something like "in my mission." Jesus wants his followers to pray for—to hunger and thirst for—those things that fit his name and his mission.

In Advent, the church grieves and awaits the return of the bodily absent Lord. Yet, in the meantime, we pray and work in the presence of the Spirit of Christ, with our lives directed toward his purposes. So, when he does come again, all of our prayerful hopes—including being reunited with him (and with those in Christ whom we love)—will come to pass, and we will rejoice, and no one will take away our joy.

BLESSING FOR THE DAY

Restore to me the joy of your salvation and grant me a willing spirit, to sustain me.

—PSALM 51:12

QUESTIONS FOR REFLECTION

1. What are the absences that you are grieving this season? Give those to God.

2. What are things we can pray for that fit "in the name" and in the will and/or mission of Jesus?

3. How can you live today acknowledging the birth pangs and aches of the old creation while also looking and praying toward the new creation with joy?

FOR THE JOY

SCRIPTURE READING

HEBREWS 12:1–3

Therefore, since we are surrounded by such a great cloud of witnesses, let us throw off everything that hinders and the sin that so easily entangles. And let us run with perseverance the race marked out for us, fixing our eyes on Jesus, the pioneer and perfecter of faith. For the joy set before him he endured the cross, scorning its shame, and sat down at the right hand of the throne of God. Consider him who endured such opposition from sinners, so that you will not grow weary and lose heart.

—HEBREWS 12:1–3

My wife is an amazing mother. She is the queen of positive re-inforcement. Because I have been in ministry during our entire marriage, I usually have to leave early and head for the church on Sundays before the rest of the family is out of bed. That has meant she's had to take on the monumental task of getting four kids ready for church and there on time. I suppose a parent could get four young kids to church with various threats and forms of coercion. It is unlikely they would grow up being glad to go to the house of the Lord, but I suppose it is possible. Fortunately, Debbie took the more positive route. There was a donut store between our home and the church, and if everyone was dressed and ready to go on time, they got to stop on the way. As the kids got older the dangling carrot of motivation was upgraded from the donut store to Starbucks, but the principle remained the same. The kids would get ready efficiently because of the vision of maple bars and chocolate milk in their minds. It was the goal toward which each Sunday morning was directed.

Ancient Greek philosophers—in particular Aristotle—called this kind of goal a *telos*. The *telos* is the target, the goal, the picture of where we want to be or what we want to accomplish that still lies out in the future ahead of us. Students study hard in order to earn a degree. Workers strive to finish a project and earn a salary. Authors push through writer's block for that wonderful day when a box of first-edition books shows up at the house. Using the metaphor from the writer of Hebrews in today's text, runners run the race with the finish line or destination in mind.

In today's text, Jesus endured his sufferings with a particular *telos* in mind: *the joy set before him*. What is the *telos* of joy set before Jesus? The writer of Hebrews doesn't articulate all that the joy of Christ means in this text, but the writer seems to assume that the reader already understands all of the joyful transformations that have taken and are taking place through the cross and resurrection. Christ endured the suffering of the cross for the joy of forming a world where good overcomes evil. Christ endured the suffering of the cross for the joy of forming a world where light overpowers darkness. Christ endured the suffering of the cross for the joy of forming a world where grace conquers sin. And Christ endured the suffering of the cross for the joy of forming a world where death is vanquished by resurrection life.

The logic of this powerful text in Hebrews is pretty straightforward. If the joyful *telos* of a world set right in God's love is the goal that helped Jesus endure the great suffering of the cross, then as we suffer and struggle in the race set before us, our *telos*, our goal, and our vision should be Christ. We run the race of our lives with our eyes fixed on Jesus and the joy we know will come when the world is set right in and through him.

Several years ago, I ran the Los Angeles Marathon and was struggling to finish with seven or eight miles still to go in the race. I was running to support a Christian organization that had made t-shirts for all of the team members with Philippians 4:13 printed on the back: *I can do all this through him who gives me strength.* A man coming up behind me in the race apparently read my t-shirt and could see I was struggling, so he came up beside me, put his hand on my shoulder, and said, "Brother, I can do all things through Christ who gives me strength. Say it with me." It was clear he wasn't going to take no for an answer. So, with as much energy as I could muster, I started repeating Philippians 4:13 with him over and over again. He invited other runners around us to join in the mantra. For about a mile a whole group of us ran chanting together, "I can do all this through him who gives me strength." A combination of faith and embarrassment helped me forget my pain, and I was able to finish the race. My new friend stayed with me until we reached the *telos*—the finish line—together. (And there was much rejoicing!)

For the writer of Hebrews, the race we run is not done alone. It is not the kind of race we run in order to finish ahead of other runners. It is the kind of race where we lose if someone fails to finish. Jesus endured the cross for the sake of the joyful *telos* of a world reconciled to God and to one another. With our eyes fixed on Jesus, our goal is not to beat others to the end. Our goal is to make sure that everyone—every tribe, nation, and language—joins in God's reconciled new creation. Only when everyone finishes this goal can we say that our joy is indeed complete.

BLESSING FOR THE DAY

Come, let us sing for joy to the Lord; let us shout aloud to the Rock of our salvation.

—PSALM 95:1

QUESTIONS FOR REFLECTION

1. What do you think of as the "joy" that Jesus accomplished in and through the cross?

   _____

   _____

   _____

   _____

2. What does it mean to you to fix your eyes upon Jesus?

   _____

   _____

   _____

   _____

3. Whom do you know who needs you to come alongside and help them finish the race today?

   _____

   _____

   _____

   _____

A RESPONSIVE READING FOR ADVENT JOY

Reader(s): We light these candles as a sign of the coming light of Christ. Advent means "coming." We are preparing for the full coming of Christ.

ALL: We are ready for Christ to come and make all things new.

Reader(s): The third candle is a symbol of joy. And the angel said unto them, "Fear not."

ALL: For behold, I bring you good tidings of great joy, which shall be to all people.

Reader(s): For unto you is born this day in the city of David,

ALL: A Savior, which is Christ the Lord.

Reader(s): When the Lord brought back the captives to Zion, we were like people who dreamed.

ALL: Our mouths were filled with laughter, our tongues with songs of joy.

Reader(s): Then it was said among the nations, "The Lord has done great things for them."

ALL: The Lord has done great things for us, and we are filled with joy.

Reader(s): Those who sow in tears will reap with songs of joy.

ALL: Those who go out weeping will return with songs of joy. For the joy of the Lord is our strength!

Reader(s): Rejoice in the Lord always! I will say it again, Rejoice!

ALL: For the Lord is near!

Reader(s): *We are preparing for the joy of the Lord to be made complete in us.*

ALL: Come quickly, Lord Jesus! We are ready for you to come and make all things new!

A FINAL PRAYER FOR ADVENT JOY

Almighty God, you have invited us to run toward joy, to endure for the sake of your joy, to weep now, knowing that joy is coming. Our joy, like yours, is found in a world set right. That joy does not come easily. It comes through labor pains. It is received through suffering. It is waited for with patience. We rejoice that Christ is making all things new. We rejoice that, because Christ suffered, sin and death have been defeated. We rejoice in expectation of the great wedding feast. Forgive us for our tendency to complain and not rejoice. Deliver us from the temptation to become cynical and despondent. Help us discern between eternal joy and temporal pleasures. May our joy draw others to you. May our joy not be complete until all others share in the joy of your reconciling love. Amen.

Jesus is a teacher who doesn't just inform our intellect but forms our very loves. He isn't content to simply deposit new ideas into your mind: he is after nothing less than your wants, your loves, your longings.

—JAMES K. A. SMITH,
You Are What You Love

There is no ceiling to love.

—MILDRED BANGS WYNKOOP,
A Theology of Love

LOVE

Fourth Sunday of Advent
December 20, 2020

SCRIPTURE READINGS

2 SAMUEL 7:1–11, 16; PSALM 89:1–4, 19–26;
LUKE 1:26–38; LUKE 1:46b–55; ROMANS 16:25–27

In the sixth month of Elizabeth's pregnancy, God sent the angel Gabriel to Nazareth, a town in Galilee, to a virgin pledged to be married to a man named Joseph, a descendant of David. The virgin's name was Mary. The angel went to her and said, "Greetings, you who are highly favored! The Lord is with you." Mary was greatly troubled at his words and wondered what kind of greeting this might be. But the angel said to her, "Do not be afraid, Mary; you have found favor with God. You will conceive and give birth to a son, and you are to call him Jesus. He will be great and will be called the Son of the Most High. The Lord God will give him the throne of his father David, and he will reign over Jacob's descendants forever; his kingdom will never end."

"How will this be," Mary asked the angel, "since I am a virgin?"

The angel answered, "The Holy Spirit will come on you, and the power of the Most High will overshadow you. So the holy one to be born will be called the Son of God. Even Elizabeth your relative is going to have a child in her old age, and she who was said to be unable to conceive is in her sixth month. For no word from God will ever fail."

"I am the Lord's servant," Mary answered. "May your word to me be fulfilled." Then the angel left her.

—LUKE 1:26–38

I have a number of personality idiosyncrasies (just ask my wife). One that my family teases me about regularly is my love of mail. I love to go to the mailbox each day, and I get a little irritated if someone else in the family beats me to it. I think the reason I love the daily mail delivery so much is that I live under a kind of illusion that one day something will arrive that will be life-changing. Maybe a large, unexpected check will come, or perhaps an invitation to a major event will arrive. Most of the time it is just a stack of bills, junk mail, and catalogues. But I remain a prisoner of hope.

The familiar text from the Gospel of Luke for today recounts the amazing, life-changing news from the angel Gabriel that Mary, a virgin, would conceive miraculously as a gift of the Holy Spirit, and give birth to a son. This news was obviously both startling and a bit overwhelming for young Mary. Luke's Gospel gives the longest and most detailed account of the birth of Jesus. The narrative is largely built on the contrast between Mary and her relative Elizabeth—and the sons they both carry in their wombs.

The story of Elizabeth and Zechariah can be read as not just an echo of God's action with Israel in the past but also as a closing of that era. Somewhat typical of the Old Testament, the story begins with the patriarch of the family, Zechariah. Elizabeth and Zechariah both come from the priestly tradition. They are described as righteous, "observing all the Lord's commands and decrees blamelessly" (1:6). Yet, despite their faithfulness, like so many of their ancestors in faith, they too were barren. The temple is the center of action, the place where Zechariah encounters Gabriel.

Their promised son, John, would live according to several practices found in the Old Testament prophetic tradition, including the avoidance of strong drink. Interestingly, this beautiful story of God's action with this barren, priestly couple ends where many of the old covenant stories also end—in muteness and in the inability to truly speak a new revelatory word from God.

In contrast, Mary is the embodiment of God's action that, although consistent with the past, brings about a whole new creation. Mary is not only a woman, but she is also essentially isolated and alone. She is not from the priestly line connected to the temple but from the kingly line connected to David. She is proclaimed as "favored," not in reference to any keeping of the law or rituals but simply because of her response in faith. Mary is not barren, but she *is* a virgin. Although Elizabeth's conception of John—like Sarah, Rachael, and Hannah before her—is miraculous, the child born of a virgin carries the significance of something altogether new. And the end result of Mary's faithfulness is not muteness but a prophetic song.

Gabriel's words to Mary—*Greetings, you who are highly favored. The Lord is with you!*—are not spoken only for her but also for the whole world. In the last week of Advent, God's people reflect on and give thanks for the love of God extended to the world in the incarnation of the Son. It is not just Mary who receives favor. It is also because "God so loves the world" (John 3:16) that the Son is sent into the world. And, because of Mary's willingness to be the instrument of God's blessing, we can also proclaim that, "The Word became flesh and made his dwelling among us" (John 1:14). God is indeed with us.

The focus of this final week of Advent is, in essence, the focus of the entire Gospel. In Christ, God extended his love to a broken and sinful world. As we, like Mary, are willing to receive that love with openness and faithfulness, we become reflections, ambassadors, and bearers of that divine love to others—a love that makes all things new.

BLESSING FOR THE DAY

Surely your goodness and love will follow me all the days of my life, and I will dwell in the house of the LORD forever.

—PSALM 23:6

HYMN FOR THE WEEK

Could we with ink the ocean fill,
And were the skies of parchment made;
Were every stalk on earth a quill,
And every man a scribe by trade;
To write the love of God above
Would drain the ocean dry.
Nor could the scroll contain the whole,
Though stretched from sky to sky.
O, Love of God, how rich and pure!
How measureless and strong!
It shall forevermore endure—
The saints' and angels' song.

QUESTIONS FOR DISCUSSION OR REFLECTION

1. What do you sense to be the new thing God wants to do in and through you this year?

   _____

   _____

   _____

   _____

2. What do you see as the contrast between what God was doing in Elizabeth and what he was doing in Mary?

   _____

   _____

   _____

3. Think of three ways that God has demonstrated his love to you.

   _____

   _____

   _____

   _____

WITH AN EVERLASTING LOVE

MONDAY, DECEMBER 21, 2020

SCRIPTURE READING

JEREMIAH 31:1–6

"At that time," declares the LORD, "I will be the God of all the families of Israel, and they will be my people." This is what the LORD says: "The people who survive the sword will find favor in the wilderness; I will come to give rest to Israel." The LORD appeared to us in the past, saying: "I have loved you with an everlasting love; I have drawn you with unfailing kindness. I will build you up again, and you, Virgin Israel, will be rebuilt. Again you will take up your timbrels and go out to dance with the joyful. Again you will plant vineyards on the hills of Samaria; the farmers will plant them and enjoy their fruit. There will be a day when watchmen cry out on the hills of Ephraim, 'Come, let us go up to Zion, to the LORD our God.'"

—JEREMIAH 31:1–6

My parents love to tell a story about me from my early childhood. I was five or six, and our family was on vacation in Estes Park, Colorado. I had (and still have) a tendency to get distracted and wander around. Apparently, while the family was going through the quaint shops downtown, I wandered away and got lost. The unusual part of the story is how I reacted. Instead of panicking, crying, and screaming for help, I simply climbed up in a planter outside the store window, crossed my legs, and calmly waited for my parents to come and find me.

I think my parents love to tell this story because, besides my tendency toward distraction, it illustrates the seeds of a calm and steady, rational nature that apparently started very early and has continued into my adulthood. In thinking more about that story recently, however, it dawned on me that the story reveals less about my natural temperament than it says about the love of my parents. What I find remarkable about the Estes Park story is that, even as young as five or six, I was convinced at the deepest part of my being that my parents loved me too much to simply walk away without me. In my young heart and mind, I knew I did not need to panic because they would be doing all they could to find me. If I just sat still and stayed calm, their love would track me down.

The majority of the book of Jeremiah is a prophetic lament about the exile of judgment coming down upon Judah and Jerusalem. In a number of outrageous ways, Jeremiah proclaimed God's tearing down of the city and all of its structures. Beginning at chapter 30, however, and extending through chapter 33, is what is often referred to as the Book of Comfort. Presumably, the Book of Comfort is a collection or scroll of hope, in the midst of judgment, centered on the promise that God will not give up on his people.

Jeremiah named the hope for the renewal of the people with three "agains:" *I will build you up **again***. The city will be reconstructed. ***Again** you will take up your timbrels and go out to dance with the joyful*. Joy and celebration will return. ***Again** you will plant vineyards . . . and enjoy their fruit*. God will again sustain them in freedom and blessing.

The people can be confident that these "agains" will come to pass because of their confidence in the *everlasting love* of God. Their wanderings have cost them a great deal. Yet they do not need to panic because the faithful and loving God will find them, will renew them, and will give them hope and a future.

BLESSING FOR THE DAY

But the eyes of the LORD are on those who fear him, on those whose hope is in his unfailing love.

May your unfailing love be with us, LORD, even as we put our hope in you.

—PSALM 33:18, 22

QUESTIONS FOR REFLECTION

1. In what ways has God demonstrated his faithful love to you recently?

    _____

    _____

    _____

    _____

2. How has God loved and found you in your wanderings?

    _____

    _____

    _____

    _____

3. Whom do you know today who is wandering and needs to be reminded of the faithful love of God? Pray for them. Ask the Lord to show you how to be a reflection of his love to them.

    _____

    _____

    _____

    _____

ABOUNDING
IN LOVE

SCRIPTURE READING

JONAH 4:1–3

But to Jonah this seemed very wrong, and he became angry. He prayed to the LORD, "Isn't this what I said, LORD, when I was still at home? That is what I tried to forestall by fleeing to Tarshish. I knew that you are a gracious and compassionate God, slow to anger and abounding in love, a God who relents from sending calamity. Now, LORD, take away my life, for it is better for me to die than to live."

—JONAH 4:1–3

When my kids were little, they loved it when I retold them familiar stories with messed-up endings. They thought it was funny when the three bears had Goldilocks arrested for trespassing (she was sentenced to community service). I had to stop, though, when I made one of them cry when the wolf ate the three pigs.

The book of Jonah is a great story with a messed-up ending. It even feels a little bit like a typical three-part children's story. First, it begins with the call on Jonah's life and him running from that call. In part two, he ends up in the belly of the fish. Then in the final act, God saves him, he preaches to Nineveh, and they repent. There should be a verse at the end of Jonah 3 that says, "And they lived happily ever after." Unfortunately, the story doesn't end at chapter 3. It goes on with the messed-up ending that is chapter 4.

In the fourth chapter, Jonah (the only representative of God's people in the whole book) completely misses out on the work of redemption and transformation that God is doing in the world's most wicked and violent city. It is not just a sad ending to Jonah's life and ministry, but I believe it is also meant to ask all of us why we keep missing out on the redemptive work God wants to see take place in the world.

The answer to why Jonah is missing out is given in the text for today, and it is a bit surprising. Although it is never plainly stated, the narrator of Jonah leaves the reader with the impression in chapter 1 that the reason Jonah fled to Tarshish was out of fear, a lack of faith, or some combination of both. However, in this text, Jonah reveals that his knowledge of how wide and deep God's love is caused him to flee.

Jonah's revealing statement is actually a quote from Exodus 34. Moses is on the mountain with God, begging to see God's glory. After getting just a glimpse, Moses pronounces what scholars call a theophany: a revelatory insight into the character of God. The theophany of Moses begins with almost the exact words from Jonah 4, but in Exodus these words are also included: "maintaining love to thousands, and forgiving wickedness, rebellion and sin. Yet he does not leave the guilty unpunished; he punishes the children and their children for the sin of the parents to the third and fourth generation" (34:7). In Jonah, this final warning has dropped out. He only speaks about God's steadfast love, not his continuing judgment. Jonah is angry because he knows that God's love for the Ninevites will trump all of the justice they *should* receive for their sin and violence (especially the sin and violence they have committed against Jonah's people). The problem for Jonah is that he and God's people have learned by the end of the Old Testament that, with God, "mercy triumphs over judgment" (James 2:13).

Toward the beginning of the Bible there is a story about how, when judgment comes, the righteous person Noah and his family float and are saved while the rest of the world sinks. The book of Jonah inverts that story and, thus, our expectations. In Jonah, the righteous person (Jonah) sinks, and the whole world—both pagan sailors and violent Ninevites—float in safety and are saved.

This is exactly the kind of inversion of imagination that Advent tries to shape in God's people. The one who had equality with God emptied himself for the sake of the world (see Philippians 2). That overwhelming love can anger us, frustrate us, and cause us to miss out (like Jonah) on everything redemptive that God wants to do in the world. Or, it can inspire us to participate in and become extensions of the transformative love of God. I am hoping, by God's grace, that our story has a better ending.

BLESSING FOR THE DAY

Your love, LORD, reaches to the heavens, your faithfulness to the skies. Your righteousness is like the highest mountains, your justice like the great deep. You, LORD, preserve both people and animals. How priceless is your unfailing love, O God! People take refuge in the shadow of your wings.

—PSALM 36:5–7

QUESTIONS FOR REFLECTION

1. Why would the love of God make Jonah angry and cause him to flee from his calling?

   _____

   _____

   _____

   _____

2. In what ways is the church still missing out on what God is doing and wants to do in the world?

   _____

   _____

   _____

   _____

3. How can we live an inverted story, believing that, like Christ, as the people of God sink into God's purposes, the world might be transformed?

   _____

   _____

   _____

   _____

WHO SHALL SEPARATE US FROM THE LOVE OF CHRIST?

WEDNESDAY, DECEMBER 23, 2020

SCRIPTURE READING

ROMANS 8:28-39

What, then, shall we say in response to these things? If God is for us, who can be against us? He who did not spare his own Son, but gave him up for us all—how will he not also, along with him, graciously give us all things?

Who shall separate us from the love of Christ? Shall trouble or hardship or persecution or famine or nakedness or danger or sword?

No, in all these things we are more than conquerors through him who loved us. For I am convinced that neither death nor life, neither angels nor demons, neither the present nor the future, nor any powers, neither height nor depth, nor anything else in all creation, will be able to separate us from the love of God that is in Christ Jesus our Lord.

—ROMANS 8:31–32, 35, 37–39

In 1 Samuel 8 the people come to Samuel, the last of the judges, and demand to have a king placed over them, so they could be like "all the other nations" (v. 5). This request makes neither Samuel nor God happy. It was God's plan after the exodus from Egypt that his people be unique in their trust of him as their Deliverer and King. Unlike the other nations, Israel was not to place their security in chariots, horses, and the trappings of kingship. God warns them that they will not like having a king, but they refuse to listen and demand to have a king placed over them. Saul becomes their first king.

What always amazes me in the story is that, just eight chapters later, God sends Samuel to Bethlehem to anoint a new king—the overlooked younger brother David. God did not want Israel to have a king. Nevertheless, rather than leave the people in their bad decision or walk away from Israel entirely, God keeps working in their midst to raise up a king after his own heart (even though he still thinks, rightly, that kings are a bad, disobedient idea).

The story of Israel's kings and God always brings to my mind Romans 8:28. This wonderful verse may be one of the most quoted and also one of the most misunderstood texts in the Bible. The promise that God is working in all things for our good can some-times lead people to think that everything that happens, no matter how evil, is intended for our good. I have had far too many people, in the most horrific moments of loss and grief, look up at me and say, "Well, we know God has a plan in this," or "We know God is trying to do something good." No! That is not what Romans 8:28 promises. Paul is not saying that everything, no matter how awful or painful, is really something good. It is not the case that God can only bring about his cosmic plan of redemption by creating moments of monumental evil and loss.

The promise is that God's love is too vast to allow evil, grief, and loss to have the last word. In all things, no matter how broken, God has the ability to lovingly work to renew, restore, and reclaim goodness if we love him and seek his purposes. Paul goes on to say that there is no hardship or distress that can separate us from the love of Christ. We know this first because Christ took on flesh and entered into our hardships. We also know this because, as he works in our lives, he can make us *more than conquerors* through his loving work.

My wife and I frequently reaffirm a promise to our four children. We don't promise to always be happy about the decisions they make in their lives. And we don't promise to withhold discipline from them when we feel it is necessary. However, we do promise that there is nothing they can do that will invalidate or take away our unconditional love for them and our desire to always work for the best in their lives regardless of the circumstances. If we, who are human, know how to make those kinds of promises to our children, how much more confident can we be that nothing *in all creation, will be able to separate us from the love of God that is in Christ Jesus our Lord?*

BLESSING FOR THE DAY

But I will sing of your strength, in the morning I will sing of your love; for you are my fortress, my refuge in times of trouble.

—PSALM 59:16

QUESTIONS FOR REFLECTION

1. What does it say about God's love that he keeps working through Israel, despite their decision contrary to his wisdom and purposes?

   _____

   _____

   _____

   _____

2. When has God brought good out of something broken in your past?

   _____

   _____

   _____

   _____

3. Why is the love of a parent so necessary for the confidence of a child? How can you live in the confidence of God's love today?

   _____

   _____

   _____

   _____

THIS IS LOVE

SCRIPTURE READING

1 JOHN 4:7–21

Dear friends, let us love one another, for love comes from God. Everyone who loves has been born of God and knows God. Whoever does not love does not know God, because God is love. This is how God showed his love among us: He sent his one and only Son into the world that we might live through him. This is love: not that we loved God, but that he loved us and sent his Son as an atoning sacrifice for our sins. Dear friends, since God so loved us, we also ought to love one another. No one has ever seen God; but if we love one another, God lives in us and his love is made complete in us.

There is no fear in love. But perfect love drives out fear, because fear has to do with punishment. The one who fears is not made perfect in love. We love because he first loved us. Whoever claims to love God yet hates a brother or sister is a liar. For whoever does not love their brother and sister, whom they have seen, cannot love God, whom they have not seen. And he has given us this command: Anyone who loves God must also love their brother and sister.

—1 JOHN 4:7–12, 18–21

I'll make you a wager. If you turn on the television right now, on December 24, within an hour there will be at least one advertisement for a diet plan, a bad-habit-breaking device, or a piece of exercise equipment. With New Year's resolutions on the horizon, companies know we are ready to make some new commitments to do better, to work harder, and to eat less. I fear that, as Advent comes to a close, we will read this beautiful and profound text about love in the spirit and through the eyes of people ready to make new resolutions.

In my preaching I try hard to avoid simple, moralistic sermons. A moralistic sermon on this epistle from John would go something like this: *Love is good and godly. You should obey the Bible and love God and your neighbor. Are you not loving God and your neighbor? Then start loving them! Are you already loving God and your neighbor? Then love them even more!* The problem with this kind of sermon or this kind of reading of 1 John is that the work—like our New Year's resolutions—depends entirely on us. However, that is not what John is saying to us. We are not simply asked to grit our teeth and try to love God and others more. There is more than a simple moralism going on here. First, John reminds us that God *is* love. The essential nature of God (and the gospel) is relational. John reminds us that the God we believe in is love.

Second, in Christ, God revealed his love to us. God's love has been revealed in many ways. The goodness of God's creation is an expression of love. God's rescuing of oppressed people reveals his love. God's patience with his people's disobedience demonstrates his love. But for John, the fullest revelation of God's love is given to us in the Son. The life, death, and resurrection of Jesus are the ultimate revelation of the deep love of God for the world.

Third, we were created to be reflections of God's love. Having been created in the image of God, as we come to know God's love more fully, we also learn to reflect that love to one another. This perfecting of the divine image of love, however, cannot be done without the gift of the Spirit to empower his love to come alive in our hearts.

Finally, we can live without fear because we understand his love. I had a theologian friend who used to love to say, "We will inevitably look like the God we believe in." I think John would agree. If we believe God is a legalistic judge, for example, then we will not only be judgmental of others, but we will also live trying to be obedient to God out of fear of his wrath and righteousness. (The Pharisees, in other words, looked just like the God they believed in.) But once we come to truly know the God who loves us so much that he dared to enter, on Christmas Eve, into our broken humanity, we will learn to live without fear and be willing to enter into the broken places around us.

My mother's best friend in life was a woman named Glaphre Gilliland. She is now with the Lord. In life, she was an amazing prayer warrior and a frequent source of God's transformation in my life and in the lives of many others. Early in my ministry, she called me one day just to check in. She asked me how things were going. I told her I was tired and gave her a long list of all the ways I was working hard to make my first ministry opportunity work and flourish. She simply responded, "You know God loves you, right?"

"Of course, Glaphre," I responded. "I know that."

She asked again. "No, Scott. I mean it. You know God loves you, right?"

I felt a little like Peter on the beach with Jesus after the resurrection (see John 21:15–19). "Of course, I know that," I said with a little irritation.

She paused. Then, with a sense of understanding and knowledge in her voice, she asked one more time, "Scott, I know you are working hard, doing good things. But you know that God loves you, right?"

I broke into tears, and the answer did not come out very clearly. In that moment she intuitively knew I was trying to prove my worthiness to a God who wanted me to know, first and foremost, that I am loved.

I hope that, whatever else Advent has been for you—an invitation to hope, to make peace, to express joy—it has also been another reminder at the depth of your being that God so loved you that he sent his only Son. The world can still often be a place of darkness, but God's love is making and will someday finally make all things new.

Let earth receive her King.

BLESSING FOR THE DAY

The LORD has made his salvation known and revealed his righteousness to the nations. He has remembered his love and his faithfulness to Israel; all the ends of the earth have seen the salvation of our God.

—PSALM 98:2–3

QUESTIONS FOR REFLECTION

1. What would it mean for you for your faith to move from moralistically working harder, to allowing God's Spirit of love to work through you?

    _____

    _____

    _____

2. How is the love of God being revealed through you? Or what does the God look like who is being revealed through you?

    _____

    _____

    _____

3. Which of the four themes of Advent—hope, peace, joy, or love—has meant the most to you this season?

    _____

    _____

    _____

A RESPONSIVE READING FOR ADVENT LOVE

Reader(s): We light these candles as a sign of the coming light of Christ. Advent means "coming." We are preparing for the full coming of Christ.

ALL: We are ready for Christ to come and make all things new.

Reader(s): The fourth candle is a symbol of love. The commandments are all summed up in this one command:

ALL: "Love your neighbor as yourself."

Reader(s): Come, glorify the Lord. In the depths of your being, rejoice in God our Savior.

ALL: God has looked with favor on the low status of his servants. He has looked on us with his faithful love.

Reader(s): From now on, we will consider our lives blessed because the Mighty One has done great things for us.

ALL: Holy is his name. He shows mercy to everyone, from one generation to the next.

Reader(s): God has shown strength with his arm. He has scattered those with arrogant thoughts and proud inclinations.

ALL: He has pulled the powerful down from their thrones and lifted up the lowly.

Reader(s): He has filled the hungry with good things and sent the rich away empty-handed.

ALL: He has come to the aid of his people. He remembers his steadfast love and mercy.

Reader(s): No one has ever seen God.

ALL: But when we love one another, his love is made complete in us.

Reader(s): We are preparing for the love of the Lord to be revealed in us.

ALL: Come quickly, Lord Jesus! We are ready for you to come and make all things new!

A FINAL PRAYER FOR ADVENT LOVE

Almighty God, you have invited us to love you and love others. We know love because you have loved us. We celebrate, in this season, divine love becoming flesh and dwelling among us. Your love is not sentimentality. You love us too much to leave us in brokenness. Your love tells the truth about our lives but also extends unmerited grace. Your love will not let us go. We are loved. Your Spirit empowers us to love. Because we are loved by you, we can risk loving others. Forgive us for our misdirected loves. We have too often learned to love the wrong things. Have mercy on us for allowing our fears to get in the way of your love. Teach us to love you fully. Help us set aside our fears so that we might love even our enemy. May the world know that there is exists a God of incarnational love because they see that love made real in and through us. Amen.